LE CREUSET®

ONE-POT CUISINE

ONE-POT CUISINE

CLASSIC RECIPES FOR CASSEROLES, TAGINES & SIMPLE ONE-POT DISHES

MITCHELL BEAZLEY

CONTENTS

A KITCHEN CLASSIC

For almost 100 years, from the company's foundry in Fresnoy-Le-Grand, in northern France, Le Creuset cookware has been created from the finest materials. The French brand has stood for the best quality in the kitchen for generations, used by top chefs and keen home cooks the world over.

Each item of Le Creuset cast iron cookware is individually hand-crafted to ensure uncompromising quality and durability. Molten iron is poured into molds to cast the shape, then cooled. Once cooled, the pot is removed from the mold and each mold is broken and recycled, meaning no two pieces of Le Creuset cookware are ever exactly the same. Each piece is then passed through the hands of 15 different skilled artisans in a meticulous 12-step finishing process, to be cleaned and smoothed, ready for enameling. The enamel provides a highly durable, hygienic, and shock-resistant finish.

Given the attention to detail devoted to the production process, it is no wonder that a Le Creuset Dutch oven, skillet grill, or stoneware pie dish can be found in the kitchen of discerning home cooks everywhere, in large country houses, contemporary apartments, and bustling family homes. Reflecting an international popularity, Le Creuset products now include the cast iron Tatin dish, the cast iron Balti dish, the Stoneware Tapas dish, and the cast iron Wok. From the trademark Volcanic orange to the more muted Chiffon Pink, classic Flint to bright Teal, everyone has their preferred color. With their flawless craftsmanship and classic style, Le Creuset products are owned with pride and affection.

So what better way to prepare delicious one-pot meals than in Le Creuset cookware? Exclusively created for the brand's famous cast iron Dutch ovens, tagines, and skillet grills, this book is bursting with more than 100 mouthwatering recipes for wonderful casseroles, tagines, and simple one-pot suppers. From slow-cooked, hearty stews to divine desserts, food for sharing on a warm, sunny day to aromatic and flavorsome tagines for an autumnal evening, there is a recipe here for every occasion.

MEAT

4½-quart Round Dutch Oven

SERVES 4 TO 6
Preparation time: 15 minutes
Cooking time: 2 hours 15 minutes

A CLASSIC BEEF CASSEROLE
Enjoy this warming casserole in the cold winter months.

2 tablespoons olive oil

1¾ lb beef for stew,
cut into 1½-inch cubes

2 large onions, cut into large pieces

4 carrots, cut into large pieces

1 parsnip, cut into large pieces

1 Granny Smith apple, peeled,
cored, and cut into ½-inch dice

2 garlic cloves, minced

2 tablespoons tomato ketchup

1 tablespoon soft light brown sugar

1 tablespoon apple cider vinegar

3 thyme sprigs

2 bay leaves

1½ cups dark ale

½ cup beef stock

2 tablespoons wholegrain mustard

1 slice of wholewheat bread

1 tablespoon cornstarch (optional)

Salt and freshly ground black pepper

Heat the oil in the Dutch oven over medium heat, add the beef, and cook until browned on all sides.

Add the onions and fry for 2 to 3 minutes. Add the carrots and parsnip, season with salt and pepper, and continue to cook for 3 to 4 minutes until the onions are soft.

Add the apple, garlic, tomato ketchup, sugar, vinegar, thyme, and bay leaves, stir, then pour in the ale. Cook for 2 minutes, stirring to release any browned bits sticking to the bottom. Pour in the stock and bring to a simmer.

Spread the mustard over one side of the bread and place it on top of the casserole, mustard side down. Cover with the lid and cook over low heat for 1½ to 2 hours until the beef is tender. If you prefer a thicker sauce, thicken the gravy by mixing the cornstarch with a little water. Stir it into the casserole toward the end of the cooking time and let cook for a further 5 minutes until thickened.

4½-quart Round Dutch Oven

SERVES 4 TO 6
Preparation time: 20 minutes
Cooking time: 2¼ hours

POT-AU-FEU MAISON

A century-old French recipe with an Italian twist.

For the gremolata:

1 garlic clove, minced

1 handful of flat-leaf parsley, chopped

Finely grated zest of 1 lemon

For the casserole:

1 tablespoon butter

1 tablespoon olive oil

1¾ lb beef for stew,
cut into 1½-inch cubes

1 tablespoon all-purpose flour

1 onion, chopped

2 bouquets garni

3 parsnips, cubed

4 carrots, cubed

½ small butternut squash, seeded and cubed (optional)

2¾ cups potatoes, cubed

3½ oz Brussels sprouts

1 cup white wine

1¼ cups beef stock

1 garlic clove, crushed

Salt and freshly ground black pepper

Preheat the oven to 350°F.

For the gremolata, mix together all the ingredients and set to one side.

Melt the butter and oil in the Dutch oven over medium heat. Dust the beef in the flour until coated, then add the meat to the butter and oil and cook until browned on all sides. Add the onion and bouquets garni and fry for 3 to 4 minutes until the onion is softened.

Add the prepared vegetables, wine, stock, and garlic and stir to combine. Season with salt and pepper. Bring the contents to a simmer and cover with the lid.

Place in the oven for 1½ to 2 hours until the beef is tender and starting to fall apart.

Serve the stew scattered with the gremolata.

Reversible Grill/Griddle

GINGER-SOY CHARGRILLED STEAK

A fragrant, Asian-inspired simple meal.

SERVES 6

Preparation time: 20 minutes, plus marinating
Cooking time: 10 minutes

3 beef steaks, such as top loin, rib-eye, or tenderloin, about 14 oz each

Olive oil, for greasing

Freshly ground black pepper

A few cilantro sprigs, to garnish

For the ginger-soy marinade:

2-inch piece fresh ginger root, peeled and thinly sliced

3 garlic cloves, thinly sliced

1 cup light soy sauce

2 tablespoons sesame oil

1½ tablespoons mirin

1 teaspoon sugar

For the Asian salad:

3 large carrots, halved and cut into long, thin strips

1 cucumber, quartered, seeded, and cut into long, thin strips

1 cup bean sprouts

Mix together all the ingredients for the ginger-soy marinade in a bowl. Reserve 2 tablespoons of the marinade to make a dressing for the Asian salad.

Season the steaks with pepper and place them in a large, nonmetallic dish. Pour the marinade over the steaks and let them marinate, covered, for at least 1 hour, turning the steaks occasionally.

For the Asian salad, combine the carrots, cucumber, and bean sprouts in a bowl and drizzle with the reserved ginger-soy marinade.

Remove the steaks from the marinade, allowing any excess to drip off. Place the reversible grill/griddle, smooth side facing upward, over high heat and grease the surface with oil. Place the steaks on the pan and cook for 3 to 5 minutes on each side, or until cooked to your liking. Remove from the pan, cover with foil, and let rest for 5 minutes.

Halve each steak, drizzle with any pan juices, and garnish with cilantro. Serve with the Asian salad.

5½-quart Round Dutch Oven

ORIENTAL-SPICED BEEF
An aromatic spiced broth transforms this beef stew into something special.

SERVES 4 TO 6
Preparation time: 15 minutes
Cooking time: 4¾ hours

3 tablespoons olive oil

2¼ lb boneless beef chuck pot roast

3 quarts beef stock

1 onion, chopped

3 lemon grass stalks

6 star anise

2 cinnamon sticks

1 to 2 mild red chiles

2-inch piece fresh ginger root,
peeled and thinly sliced

1 tablespoon whole
black peppercorns

4 cloves

1 tablespoon sugar

2 tablespoons soy sauce

1 tablespoon fish sauce

1¼ cups cooked rice noodles

1 handful of cilantro,
leaves coarsely chopped, divided

1¼ cups bean sprouts

4½ oz small shiitake mushrooms,
finely chopped

3 scallions, chopped

2 limes, cut into wedges

Heat the oil in the Dutch oven over medium heat, add the beef chuck, and brown it on all sides. Remove the beef from the pot and set aside. Add the stock to the pot and stir to release any browned bits sticking to the bottom. Bring to a simmer, then return the beef to the pot.

Add the onion, lemon grass, star anise, cinnamon sticks, chiles, and ginger to the stock mixture. Place the peppercorns and cloves in an infuser or tie in a small piece of cheesecloth and add to the pot. Stir in the sugar, soy sauce, and fish sauce. Cover with the lid and simmer over low heat for 4 to 4½ hours until the beef is tender. If needed, add extra soy sauce, to taste, at the end of the cooking time.

Remove the spices and slice the beef. Place the rice noodles, half of the cilantro leaves, bean sprouts, shiitake mushrooms, and scallions in individual serving bowls. Top each with the sliced beef and add some broth.

Scatter each serving with the remaining cilantro, along with a squeeze of lime juice.

VEAL WITH FAVA BEANS & MINT

This springtime tagine is fresh, vibrant, and light.

2-quart Tagine

SERVES 4
Preparation time: 15 minutes
Cooking time: 1¾ hours

2 tablespoons olive oil

1¾ lb leg (round) of veal, cut into 4 pieces

2 small onions, minced

¾ cup water

1 teaspoon ground cumin

1 bunch of flat-leaf parsley, tied together with kitchen string

1 lb 2 oz fava beans, shelled

3 mint sprigs, leaves chopped, divided

Salt and freshly ground black pepper

Heat the oil in the bottom of the tagine over medium heat, add the veal, and brown on all sides. Add the onions and fry for 5 minutes until soft.

Add the measured water, cumin, and parsley and season with salt and pepper. Bring to a simmer, reduce the heat to low, and cover with the lid. Cook the veal for 1½ hours, or until tender.

Stir the fava beans into the tagine with half of the mint. Replace the lid and simmer gently for another 10 minutes or until the beans are cooked.

Serve the tagine scattered with the remaining mint.

NOTE: *If you want to remove the outer shell from the fava beans, blanch them first, then drain and immerse in ice-cold water to stop them from cooking further. Squeeze the beans out of their gray outer shell and set them aside until needed. Add the beans 5 minutes before the end of the cooking time.*

VEAL CUTLETS WITH TOMATO & MOZZARELLA

The fragrant flavors of Italy on a plate.

9½-inch Oval Cast Iron Dish

SERVES 4
Preparation time: 10 minutes
Cooking time: 25 minutes

8 tomatoes

1 teaspoon olive oil

4 veal leg cutlets

2 onions, minced

1 garlic clove, finely chopped

4 sage leaves

9 oz mozzarella cheese,
drained and sliced

Salt and freshly ground black pepper

Preheat the oven to 325°F.

To skin the tomatoes, put them in a bowl and add boiling water to cover. Let stand for 1 to 2 minutes, then drain, cut a cross at the stem end of each tomato, and peel off the skin. Cut the tomatoes into thick slices.

Heat the oil in the cast iron dish over medium heat, add the veal cutlets, and cook briefly until browned on each side. Remove from the dish, season with salt and pepper, and keep warm.

Turn the heat to low, add the onions and garlic to the dish, and fry for 5 minutes until soft, then move the mixture to one side of the dish.

Lay the tomatoes in the dish, and place a veal cutlet on each. Spoon the onions and garlic on top, and then add a sage leaf to each cutlet. Season with salt and pepper, and finish with the mozzarella.

Place the dish in the oven for 20 minutes, or until the mozzarella melts and starts to turn golden.

Serve with pasta, if you like, cooked al dente.

4½-quart Round Dutch Oven

CREAMY VEAL RAGOUT

A delicious classic recipe of veal, served two ways, in a creamy sauce.

SERVES 6
Preparation time: 20 minutes
Cooking time: 1¾ hours

1 lb 2 oz boneless veal, cut
into 1½-inch cubes

3 carrots, sliced

2 onions, chopped

2 leeks, sliced

3 celery stalks, sliced

20 pearl onions or small shallots, peeled

20 baby mushrooms, cut in half

1 bouquet garni

2 to 3 cloves

1 cup veal or light beef stock

2 tablespoons butter

3 tablespoons flour

1 cup heavy cream

2 egg yolks

Juice of ½ lemon

Salt and freshly ground black pepper

1 bunch of flat-leaf parsley, chopped,
to garnish

For the meatballs:

9 oz ground veal

1 egg, lightly beaten

2 tablespoons fresh bread crumbs

3 flat-leaf parsley sprigs,
leaves finely chopped

2 tablespoons vegetable oil, divided

For the meatballs, mix the ground veal with the egg, bread crumbs, and chopped parsley. With wet hands, form the mixture into walnut-sized meatballs.

Heat 1 tablespoon of the oil in the Dutch oven over medium heat, add the meatballs, and cook until browned all over. Then remove with a slotted spoon and set aside.

For the casserole, add the remaining oil and the cubed veal to the Dutch oven and brown on all sides, then remove with slotted spoon.

Add the carrots, onions, leeks, celery, onions or shallots, mushrooms, bouquet garni, and cloves and fry for 5 minutes until the vegetables have softened.

Return the meatballs and veal to the Dutch oven and add the stock along with enough water to cover. Bring to a boil, reduce the heat to low, cover with the lid, and let simmer gently for 1 to 1¼ hours until the meat is tender. Remove the meatballs, veal, and vegetables from the Dutch oven using a slotted spoon, cover, and set aside. Strain the stock into a pitcher and set aside.

Melt the butter in the Dutch oven. Add the flour and cook, stirring, for 1 minute. Pour in the stock, a little at a time, stirring constantly. Bring to a simmer and cook the sauce for 5 minutes until smooth and thickened. Mix together the cream and egg yolks and stir the mixture into the sauce.

Return the meatballs, veal, and vegetables to the sauce and heat through gently, stirring, then add the lemon juice and season with salt and pepper.

Scatter with the parsley and serve with crusty bread or brown rice.

LEBANESE-STYLE MEATBALLS

Meatballs with fresh mint in an aromatic spiced tomato sauce.

4½-quart Round Dutch Oven

SERVES 6
Preparation time: 25 minutes
Cooking time: 40 minutes

For the meatballs:

9 oz ground beef

9 oz ground pork

½ small onion, minced

3 tablespoons fresh white bread crumbs

1 egg, lightly beaten

1 tablespoon finely chopped mint leaves

A pinch of cayenne pepper

½ teaspoon salt

½ teaspoon freshly ground black pepper

2 to 3 tablespoons flour

½ tablespoon butter

¼ cup olive oil, divided

For the tomato sauce:

1 small red onion, minced

2 garlic cloves, crushed

2 x 14 oz cans diced tomatoes

1 tablespoon balsamic vinegar

1 teaspoon paprika

½ teaspoon ground cinnamon

½ teaspoon ground cloves

1 teaspoon sugar

3 ½ oz sun-dried tomatoes, chopped

½ oz goat cheese, crumbled

2 teaspoons tomato paste

Salt and freshly ground black pepper

Basil leaves, to garnish

For the meatballs, combine the ground beef and pork with the onion, bread crumbs, egg, mint, cayenne, salt, and pepper. Dust your hands with flour and form the mixture into walnut-sized meatballs.

Melt the butter and half of the oil in the Dutch oven over medium heat. Add the meatballs and brown them all over, then remove them from the pot with a slotted spoon and set aside.

To make the tomato sauce, heat the remaining oil in the Dutch oven over medium heat, add the red onion and garlic, and fry for 3 minutes until soft.

Add the tomatoes, vinegar, paprika, cinnamon, cloves, and sugar. Season with salt and pepper. Cover with the lid and cook over low heat for 15 minutes, stirring regularly.

Stir the sun-dried tomatoes, goat cheese, tomato paste, and browned meatballs into the sauce. Simmer over medium-low heat for 10 to 15 minutes, stirring occasionally, until the sauce has reduced and thickened.

Scatter with basil leaves and serve with pasta, if liked.

BAKED MEATBALLS WITH CHERRY SAUCE

Baked in the oven until golden, these meatballs are served with a fruity sweet cherry sauce.

9-inch Square Stoneware Dish

SERVES 4
Preparation time: 15 minutes
Cooking time: 30 minutes

---

14 oz ground veal

14 oz ground pork

1 shallot, minced

1 small handful of flat-leaf parsley, leaves chopped

2 eggs

2 tablespoons bread crumbs

1½ tablespoons butter

2 thyme sprigs

Salt and freshly ground black pepper

For the sweet cherry sauce:

1¼ cups frozen, pitted sweet cherries

2 tablespoons water

2 teaspoons superfine sugar

1½ teaspoons cornstarch

Preheat the oven to 325°F.

Mix together the ground veal and pork, shallot, parsley, eggs, and bread crumbs. Season with salt and pepper. With wet hands, form the mixture into walnut-sized meatballs.

Grease the stoneware dish with the butter, add the meatballs in an even layer, and top with the thyme. Bake the meatballs for 30 minutes until golden and cooked through. Check regularly, turning the meatballs and basting them with any juices in the bottom of the dish.

To make the cherry sauce, put the frozen cherries and measured water in a microwaveable bowl and cook on high for 2 to 3 minutes, or until defrosted and heated through. Remove the bowl from the microwave and add the sugar. Mix the cornstarch into a splash of hot water and stir it into the cherries to combine. Return the bowl to the microwave for another 1 to 2 minutes until heated through and thickened. Remove from the microwave and stir well, adding a splash more water if needed. Crush the cherries with the back of a fork to make a smoother sauce, if liked.

Serve the meatballs with the cherry sauce on the side.

Cast Iron Rectangular Grill

PORK CHOPS IN ROSÉ WITH ROSEMARY & ANCHOVIES
This dish captures the aromas and flavors of the south of France.

SERVES 6

Preparation time: 10 minutes, plus marinating
Cooking time: 10 minutes

6 to 8 canned anchovy fillets, drained

3 garlic cloves

2 rosemary sprigs, leaves picked and stems discarded

3 tablespoons olive oil

⅔ cup rosé

6 pork chops, about 9 oz each

Salt and freshly ground black pepper

Mash the anchovies with the garlic, rosemary leaves, and a little salt and pepper into a coarse paste. Add the oil and rosé and stir until combined.

Place the pork chops in a nonmetallic dish and spoon the marinade over them. Let marinate, covered, in the refrigerator for 3 hours, turning the chops occasionally. Remove the pork from the refrigerator 30 minutes before cooking.

Heat the skillet grill over high heat. Grill the pork chops for 5 minutes on each side, or until cooked to your liking. (You will have to cook the pork in two batches.) Remove the pork from the pan to a warm plate, cover with foil, and let rest for 10 minutes.

The pork is delicious served with mashed potatoes and green beans.

2-quart Tagine

SERVES 6
Preparation time: 15 minutes
Cooking time: 1¼ hours

HERB-STUFFED PORK BELLY
Pork stuffed with fragrant herbs and cooked in a tagine with white wine.

2¾ lb pork belly, rind removed

1 tablespoon thyme, chopped

1 tablespoon rosemary, chopped

1 tablespoon sage, chopped

1 bunch of flat-leaf parsley, leaves chopped

2 tablespoons olive oil

3 shallots, minced

3 garlic cloves, chopped

1 cup dry white wine

2 bay leaves

2¼ lb precooked Swiss chard

Light soy sauce to taste

Salt and freshly ground black pepper

Season the pork all over with salt and pepper. Spread the chopped herbs over the underside of the pork belly and roll it up to enclose the herbs. Secure in place with kitchen string; tie in several places using butcher's knots.

Heat 1 tablespoon of the oil in the bottom of the tagine over medium heat, add the rolled pork, and cook until browned on all sides. Remove the pork and set aside.

Add the remaining oil to the tagine and fry the shallots and garlic for 3 to 5 minutes until soft.

Pour in the white wine, add the bay leaves, and let simmer gently for 2 to 3 minutes. Reduce the heat to very low, place the rolled pork in the tagine, cover with the lid, and cook for 1 hour, or until the pork is tender.

Add the cooked chard to the tagine, along with a good splash of soy sauce. Continue to cook for 20 minutes, checking occasionally that there is enough moisture in the tagine. Add water as required.

Remove the pork, cover with foil, and let rest for 5 minutes. Place the rested meat on a board, remove the string and cut into slices.

Return the sliced pork with any juices to the tagine, ready to serve.

5-quart Oval Dutch Oven

SERVES 6
Preparation time: 15 minutes
Cooking time: 50 minutes

PORK TENDERLOIN WITH HERB SAUCE

The abundance of fresh herbs gives a flavor boost to this simple pork dish.

---

2 pork tenderloins, about ¾ to 1 lb each

2 tablespoons olive oil

4 curry leaf sprigs

4 oregano sprigs

4 rosemary sprigs

4 thyme sprigs

Strips of peel and juice of 1 orange

1 tablespoon butter

For the herb sauce:

1¾ cups beef stock

⅔ cup dry white wine

1 shallot, minced

¼ cup chopped mixed herbs, such as curry leaves, oregano, rosemary, and thyme

2 to 3 teaspoons cornstarch mixed with 1 tablespoon water

½ stick ice-cold butter, diced

Salt and freshly ground black pepper

Preheat the oven to 350°F.

Season the pork tenderloins with salt and pepper. Place them together and secure in several places with kitchen string.

Heat the oil in the Dutch oven over medium heat, add the pork, and brown all over. Remove the pork and set aside.

Place the herb sprigs and orange peel in the Dutch oven and place the pork on top. Pour the orange juice evenly over the meat and dot the top with the butter. Cover with the lid and place in the oven for 30 to 35 minutes until the meat is cooked through (the timing will depend on the thickness of the meat).

Remove the Dutch oven from the oven, place the pork on a warmed plate, cover with foil, and let rest for 10 minutes.

While the pork is resting, prepare the herb sauce. Remove the herbs and orange from the Dutch oven and wipe it clean. Add the beef stock, wine, and minced shallot to the Dutch oven and bring to a boil. Add the chopped herbs, then reduce the heat and simmer until the liquid has reduced by one-third.

Strain the herb sauce through a sieve and then return it to the Dutch oven. Place over low heat, add the cornstarch mixture, and stir until the sauce has thickened slightly. Stir in the diced butter, season with salt and pepper, and pour the sauce into a warmed gravy boat.

Place the rested meat on a board, remove the string, and cut the meat into slices. To serve, arrange the pork on plates, drizzle it with any pan juices, and accompany with the herb sauce.

Spring vegetables are the perfect accompaniment to the pork.

2-quart Tagine

SERVES 2 TO 3
Preparation time: 15 minutes
Cooking time: 1 hour 10 minutes

CHORIZO & CELERY ROOT ONE-POT

Despite its Spanish influence, this simple one-pot meal of chorizo and celery root is cooked in a tagine.

2 tablespoons olive oil

2 small red onions, cut into thin rings

1 lb 2 oz celery root, cut into thick slices and halved

1 cup water

2 bay leaves

A few thyme sprigs

7 oz cooking chorizo sausages

Salt and freshly ground black pepper

1 small bunch of flat-leaf parsley, leaves coarsely chopped, to garnish

Heat the oil in the bottom of the tagine over medium heat, add the onions, and sauté for 10 minutes until lightly caramelized.

Add the celery root, the measured water, bay leaves, and thyme and place the chorizo sausages on top. Reduce the heat to low, cover with the lid, and cook for 1 hour, or until the celery root is tender.

Season with salt and pepper and scatter with the parsley just before serving.

Square Griddle with Double Handles

SERVES 2
Preparation time: 15 minutes
Cooking time: 25 minutes

SPANISH CHORIZO WITH EGGS & MANCHEGO

In Spain, Manchego cheese is often served as part of tapas. Here, it is integrated into a wholesome griddled dish.

---

2 bell peppers (any color), seeded and sliced

Olive oil, for brushing

2½ oz spicy chorizo, sliced

1 small red onion, thickly sliced

8 cherry tomatoes, cut in half

2 eggs

½ teaspoon paprika

1 teaspoon Provençal spices

1½ oz Manchego cheese, grated, plus extra to serve

Salt and freshly ground black pepper

Brush the sliced bell peppers with a little oil. Heat the nonstick griddle over high heat, lightly grease with oil, add the bell peppers, and grill for 10 minutes, turning once, until starting to blacken.

Turn the heat down to medium, add the chorizo and onion, and cook for 5 minutes until the onion starts to color. Add the cherry tomatoes and cook for 3 minutes until softened slightly. Season with salt and pepper.

Make two holes in the vegetable mixture and crack an egg into each one. Sprinkle with paprika, Provençal spices, and the Manchego.

Cover the griddle with a fitted lid or foil; make sure that the foil does not touch the peppers. Cook for 5 to 7 minutes over low heat until the eggs are cooked through. Serve with extra Manchego on the side.

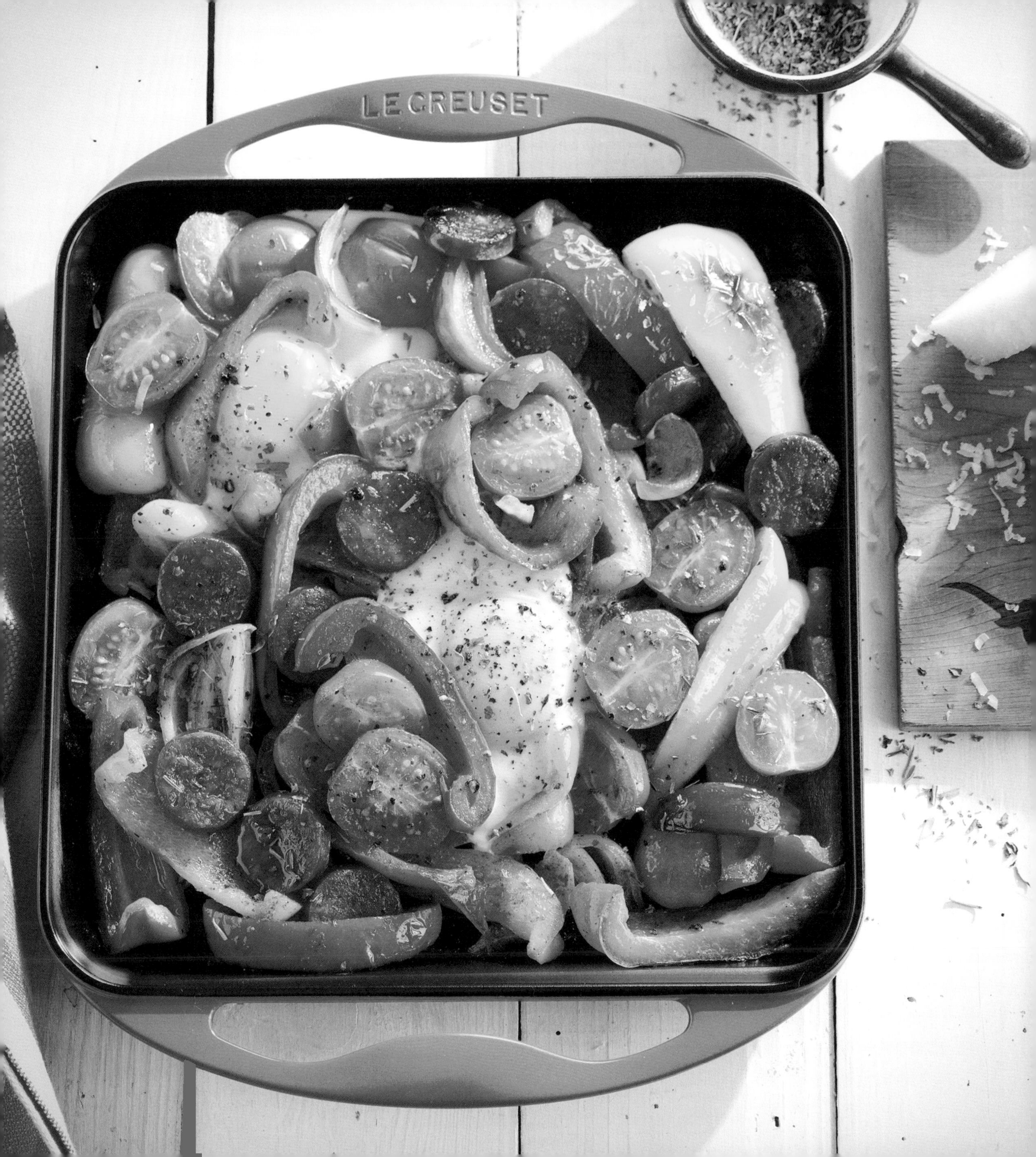
LE CREUSET

MEDITERRANEAN SAUSAGE CASSEROLE

A hearty meal influenced by Mediterranean-style cooking.

2- or 4½-quart Round Dutch Oven

SERVES 4
Preparation time: 10 minutes
Cooking time: 45 minutes

1 tablespoon olive oil

8 thick pork sausages, pricked

1 onion, chopped

1 each red, green, and yellow bell pepper, seeded and cut into large pieces

2 celery stalks, coarsely diced

2 garlic cloves, crushed

3 thyme sprigs

3 oregano sprigs

1½ teaspoons paprika

½ teaspoon cayenne pepper

1 tablespoon red wine vinegar

1 tablespoon all-purpose flour

3 cups chicken stock

1 x 14 oz can diced tomatoes

Salt and freshly ground black pepper

Finely chopped scallions and flat-leaf parsley, to garnish

Heat the oil in the Dutch oven over medium heat, add the sausages, and cook until browned all over. Remove the sausages from the Dutch oven and set aside.

Add the onion, bell peppers, and celery to the Dutch oven and fry for 10 to 12 minutes until softened. Add the garlic, thyme, oregano, and spices and fry for another 2 to 3 minutes. Add the vinegar and flour and cook, stirring, for 1 to 2 minutes.

Return the sausages to the Dutch oven. Stir in the chicken stock and diced tomatoes, and season with salt and pepper. Bring to a simmer and cook for 15 minutes until the sauce has reduced and thickened.

Serve the casserole scattered with chopped scallions and parsley.

Try serving with crusty bread for mopping up the sauce.

2-quart Tagine

SERVES 4
Preparation time: 15 minutes, plus soaking
Cooking time: 3 hours

SAUSAGES WITH WHITE BEANS, RED BELL PEPPER & SAFFRON

A warming supper dish for the cold winter months.

1 cup dry white beans, such as cannellini or navy beans

2 large tomatoes

2 tablespoons duck fat

4 thick pork sausages

2 small onions, chopped

4½ oz diced bacon

2 garlic cloves, crushed

½ large red bell pepper, seeded and cut into small dice

1 teaspoon mild smoked paprika

A pinch of saffron threads

1 bouquet garni

1 cup water, plus extra if needed

Salt and freshly ground black pepper

½ bunch of flat-leaf parsley, leaves coarsely chopped, to garnish

Place the beans in a large bowl, cover with cold water, and let soak overnight. Drain and rinse the beans.

To skin the tomatoes, put them in a bowl and add boiling water to cover. Let stand for 1 to 2 minutes, then drain, cut a cross at the stem end of each tomato, and peel off the skin. Dice the tomatoes and set aside.

Heat 1 tablespoon of the duck fat in the bottom of the tagine over medium heat, add the sausages, and cook until browned all over. Remove the sausages and set aside.

Add the remaining duck fat to the bottom of the tagine and fry the onions and bacon, stirring occasionally, for 10 minutes, or until lightly golden. Add the garlic, red bell pepper, diced tomatoes, paprika, and saffron and stir well. Reduce the heat to low, cover with the lid, and cook for 10 minutes.

Stir the white beans, bouquet garni, and the measured water into the sauce. Reduce the heat to very low, replace the lid, and cook for 2½ hours, or until the beans are tender. Check occasionally to see if there is enough moisture in the tagine and, if needed, add extra water as required.

Season with salt and pepper and stir in the browned sausages. Replace the lid and cook gently for a further 20 minutes, or until the sausages are cooked through. Scatter with chopped parsley to serve.

4½-quart Round Dutch Oven

SERVES 6
Preparation time: 15 minutes
Cooking time: 40 minutes

CASSOULET

Bring the Pyrenees into your home with this rich, hearty cassoulet.

3 tomatoes

½ tablespoon vegetable oil

9 oz ham, cut into pieces

9 oz sausages, pricked

3½ oz smoked sausage, skin removed, sliced

2 onions, chopped

2 garlic cloves, crushed

1 x 14 oz can white beans, drained

1 x 7 oz can red beans, drained

1 x 8½ oz can lima beans, drained

½ cup dry white wine

2 bay leaves

4 cloves

2 tablespoons tomato paste

2 teaspoons mustard

1 tablespoon molasses

Salt and freshly ground black pepper

To skin the tomatoes, put them in a bowl and add boiling water to cover. Let stand for 1 to 2 minutes, then drain, cut a cross at the stem end of each tomato and peel off the skin. Dice the tomatoes and set aside.

Heat the oil in the Dutch oven over medium heat, add the ham, sausages, and smoked sausage and cook until browned all over. Season the meat with pepper, then remove it from the Dutch oven and set aside.

Add the onions and garlic to the Dutch oven and fry for 2 to 3 minutes until lightly colored. Stir in the diced tomatoes along with the beans, wine, bay leaves, cloves, tomato paste, mustard, and molasses. Return the meat to the Dutch oven and bring to a simmer. Cover with the lid and cook over low heat for 20 minutes.

Take the cassoulet out of the oven and remove the bay leaves and cloves, ready to serve.

PORK CHEEKS IN DARK ALE
Here, this economical cut of pork is turned into something special.

4½-quart Round Dutch Oven

SERVES 4
Preparation time: 15 minutes
Cooking time: 1¾ hours

3 tablespoons butter, divided

3½ cups quartered mushrooms

1 tablespoon olive oil

1¾ lb pork cheeks, trimmed

2 onions, chopped

1 tablespoon flour

1 cup dark ale

½ cup beef stock

1 thyme sprig

2 bay leaves

Salt and freshly ground black pepper

Preheat the oven to 325°F.

Heat half the butter in the Dutch oven over medium heat, add the mushrooms, and fry for 8 minutes until starting to brown and there is no trace of liquid remaining. Remove the mushrooms with a slotted spoon and set aside.

Heat the remaining butter and the oil in the Dutch oven over medium heat, add the pork cheeks, and brown them all over. Remove from the pot and set aside.

Add the onions and fry until lightly caramelized, then season with salt and pepper. Stir in the flour and cook for 1 minute, then add the ale, stock, thyme, and bay leaves. Return the pork cheeks to the Dutch oven and stir until combined.

Cover with the lid—or, if desired, transfer to a stoneware dish (as shown) and cover with foil—and place in the oven for 1½ hours, or until the pork cheeks are tender. Stir the mushrooms into the mixture for the last 5 minutes of cooking and warm through.

Delicious served Belgian-style with freshly cooked french fries.

2-quart Tagine

SERVES 4
Preparation time: 15 minutes, plus soaking
Cooking time: 2½ hours

LAMB WITH APRICOTS, RAISINS & CHICKPEAS

A lightly spiced lamb tagine with fruit, chickpeas, and fresh cilantro.

½ cup dried chickpeas

1 tablespoon olive oil

1¼ lb boned lamb leg or shoulder, cut into 1-inch cubes

2 onions, chopped

A generous pinch of saffron threads

¼ teaspoon ground ginger

⅓ cinnamon stick

1 cup water, plus extra if needed

1¼ cups pitted, halved fresh apricots (or 8 dried apricots, cut in half)

¼ cup raisins

1 teaspoon honey

1 small bunch of cilantro, leaves coarsely chopped, divided

Salt and freshly ground black pepper

Place the dried chickpeas in a large bowl, cover with cold water, and let soak overnight. Drain and rinse the beans.

Heat the oil in the bottom of the tagine over medium heat, add the lamb, and brown on all sides. Remove the lamb with a slotted spoon and set aside.

Add the onions to the bottom of the tagine and fry until lightly caramelized.

Return the browned lamb to the tagine, stir in the saffron, ginger, cinnamon stick, and the drained chickpeas and add the measured water. Bring to a simmer then reduce the heat to low, cover with the lid, and cook for 2 hours, or until the lamb and chickpeas are tender. Check occasionally that there is enough moisture in the tagine and, if necessary, add some extra water.

Stir the apricots, raisins, honey, and half of the cilantro leaves into the tagine. Season with salt and pepper. (Only add salt once the chickpeas are cooked.) Continue to cook over low heat with the lid on for 20 minutes.

Serve the tagine scattered with the remaining cilantro.

3¾-quart Braiser

SERVES 4
Preparation time: 20 minutes
Cooking time: 1 hour 10 minutes

LAMB NAVARIN

A lightly spiced version of the classic, slow-cooked French casserole.

1 tablespoon butter

2 tablespoons olive oil

1¾ lb boned lamb shoulder or neck, cut into 1-inch cubes

½ teaspoon salt

1 teaspoon black pepper

1 tablespoon all-purpose flour

1 cup light ale with a squeeze of lemon, or lemon Belgian beer

1 shallot, minced

2 garlic cloves, crushed

1 oz piece fresh ginger root, peeled and finely chopped

2 carrots, cut into ¾-inch dice

7 oz fine green beans, trimmed

1¼ cups canned chickpeas, drained

1 cup vegetable stock

2 teaspoons ground coriander

2 teaspoons ground cumin

2 teaspoons caraway seeds

½ teaspoon ground cinnamon

A pinch of saffron threads

1 tablespoon honey

Salt and freshly ground black pepper

⅓ cup coarsely chopped mint, to garnish

⅓ cup coarsely chopped cilantro, to garnish

Heat the butter and oil in the braiser over medium heat, add the lamb, and brown on all sides. Stir in the salt and pepper.

Sprinkle the lamb with the flour and cook, stirring, for 1 minute. Add the ale or beer, stir to release any brown bits sticking to the bottom of the braiser, and cook until reduced.

Add the shallot, garlic, ginger, carrots, and green beans to the braiser. Stir in the chickpeas, vegetable stock, and spices. Cover with the lid and cook slowly for 45 minutes to 1 hour, stirring occasionally, until the lamb is tender.

Stir in the honey and season to taste. Just before serving, scatter with the fresh herbs.

You could serve this dish with toasted pitta bread.

2-quart Tagine

SERVES 4
Preparation time: 20 minutes
Cooking time: 55 minutes

LAMB KEFTA IN TOMATO SAUCE WITH BAKED EGGS

Aromatic spiced meatballs with eggs and cooked in a fresh tomato sauce.

For the lamb kefta:

1 lb 2 oz lean ground lamb

1 large onion, chopped, divided

½ bunch of cilantro, leaves chopped, plus extra to garnish

6 mint leaves, chopped

1 teaspoon mild chili powder

A pinch of allspice

A pinch of ground cinnamon

½ teaspoon ground cumin

2 tablespoons olive oil, divided

For the tagine:

9 oz fresh tomatoes

½ teaspoon ground ginger

½ teaspoon ground cumin

½ bunch of flat-leaf parsley, leaves chopped

½ cup water

4 eggs

Salt and freshly ground black pepper

For the lamb kefta, mix the ground lamb with half the chopped onion, the cilantro, mint, chili powder, allspice, cinnamon, and cumin. Season with a pinch of salt. With wet hands, form the mixture into small balls, roughly 1¼ inches in diameter.

Heat 1 tablespoon of the oil in the bottom of the tagine and brown the meatballs on all sides. Remove from the tagine with a slotted spoon and set aside.

For the tagine, first skin the tomatoes. Put them in a bowl and add boiling water to cover. Leave for 1 to 2 minutes, then drain, cut a cross at the stem end of each tomato and peel off the skin. Dice the tomatoes and set aside.

Heat the remaining oil in the bottom of the tagine and fry the reserved half of the chopped onion over low heat until translucent. Add the diced tomato, ginger, cumin, parsley, and the measured water. Bring the sauce to a simmer, then reduce the heat to low and cook for 20 minutes. Season to taste with salt and pepper.

Add the meatballs to the sauce, cover with the lid, and simmer over medium-low heat for 20 minutes until cooked through.

Reduce the heat to the lowest temperature, make 4 dips spaced well apart in the sauce, and break an egg into each one. Replace the lid and continue to cook for 5 minutes until the eggs are cooked. Garnish with cilantro and serve immediately.

5-quart Oval Dutch Oven

SERVES 4
Preparation time: 15 minutes
Cooking time: 1 hour 20 minutes

LEG OF LAMB WITH LENTILS
Lamb, figs and lentils, a heartwarming combination.

1¼ lb leg of lamb, boned

1 tablespoon olive oil

1 tablespoon butter

2 shallots, chopped

1 garlic clove, crushed

1 carrot, finely diced

⅔ cup red wine

1⅓ cups dry Puy lentils, rinsed

3 cups vegetable stock

2 bay leaves

2 to 3 fresh sage sprigs

4 fresh figs, cut in half

2 to 3 flat-leaf parsley sprigs,
leaves chopped

A dash of apple cider vinegar

Salt and freshly ground
black pepper

Season the lamb with salt and pepper.

Heat the oil and butter in the Dutch oven over medium heat, add the lamb, and brown on all sides. Remove the lamb and cover with foil to keep it warm.

Add the shallots, garlic, and carrot and cook in the juices from the meat for 5 minutes, stirring. Pour in the red wine and cook until reduced, stirring to release any brown bits sticking to the bottom.

Stir in the lentils, stock, bay leaves, and sage and bring to a boil over medium heat. Then reduce the heat and simmer for 10 minutes. Add the browned lamb and the figs. Cover with the lid and cook over low heat for 40 to 50 minutes until the lentils and the meat are cooked. Check toward the end of the cooking time and add a little water if the mixture has become too dry.

Take the meat out of the Dutch oven and let it rest for 5 to 10 minutes. Stir the parsley and vinegar into the lentils and season with salt and pepper. Slice the lamb and serve it with the lentils.

2-quart Tagine

SERVES 6
Preparation time: 15 minutes
Cooking time: 2¼ hours

LAMB WITH PRUNES, ALMONDS & HONEY
A classic Moroccan tagine, full of flavor.

2 tablespoons olive oil, divided

2¾ lb boned lamb leg or shoulder, cut into 12 pieces

2 large onions, sliced

1 garlic clove, chopped

A pinch of saffron threads

1 teaspoon ground ginger

2 cinnamon sticks

1 cup water, plus extra as required

10½ oz Agen prunes

2 tablespoons honey

½ teaspoon ground cinnamon

1½ tablespoons butter

⅓ cup toasted almonds, skins removed

2 tablespoons toasted sesame seeds

Salt and freshly ground black pepper

Heat 1 tablespoon of the oil in the bottom of the tagine over medium heat and add half of the lamb. Brown it on all sides, then set aside. Repeat with the remaining lamb and set aside.

Add the second tablespoon of oil and the onions to the bottom of the tagine and fry until the onions are lightly caramelized.

Stir in the garlic and return the browned pieces of lamb to the tagine. Sprinkle with the saffron and ginger, add the cinnamon sticks, and season with salt and pepper.

Add the measured water and bring to a boil. Cover with the lid, then reduce the heat to very low and cook for 1 hour. Stir in the prunes, honey, ground cinnamon, and butter. Cover and cook for a further 1 hour, or until the lamb is tender. Check occasionally that there is enough moisture in the tagine and, if necessary, add extra water as required.

Ten minutes before the end of the cooking time, stir in the toasted almonds and adjust the seasoning to taste. Scatter with the toasted sesame seeds and serve.

NOTE: *The bottom of the tagine placed over low heat can be used to toast nuts and seeds.*

POULTRY & GAME

4½-quart Round Dutch Oven

SERVES 4
Preparation time: 15 minutes
Cooking time: 1¾ hours

COQ AU VIN BLANC

A twist on the classic chicken dish with a rich, creamy white wine sauce.

2¼ lb whole chicken, cut into quarters

1 tablespoon vegetable oil

2 tablespoons butter

1¾ oz bacon, cut into ½-inch dice

2 shallots, minced

1 garlic clove, minced

9 oz baby mushrooms, cut into quarters

1 tablespoon all-purpose flour

1 cup sherry

2 cups dry white wine

3 large tomatoes, seeded and diced

2 bay leaves

3 thyme sprigs

½ cup heavy cream

Salt and freshly ground black pepper

Season the chicken portions with salt and pepper and set aside.

Heat the oil and butter in the Dutch oven over medium heat, add the diced bacon, and fry until golden.

Stir in the shallots, garlic, and mushrooms and continue to fry for 3 to 4 minutes until the vegetables are soft. Remove everything from the Dutch oven with a slotted spoon, leaving the oil behind.

Add the chicken to the hot oil and brown it on all sides. Sprinkle with the flour and stir. Pour in the sherry and wine and cook until reduced, stirring to release any brown bits sticking to the bottom. Add the tomatoes, bay leaves, and thyme and bring to a boil.

Return the bacon, shallots, garlic, and mushrooms to the Dutch oven, then reduce the heat to low, cover with the lid, and simmer for 1 hour, stirring occasionally, until the chicken is tender.

Remove the lid, take out and discard the bay leaves, and cook for a further 30 minutes, adding some water if the sauce is too dry, until the chicken is cooked through. Stir in the cream and warm through just before serving.

NOTE: *Ask your butcher to cut up the chicken for you.*

2-quart Tagine

CHICKEN WITH CARAMELIZED APPLES
Succulent spiced chicken with caramelized apples and crunchy sesame seeds.

SERVES 3
Preparation time: 15 minutes
Cooking time: 1¾ hours

1 tablespoon olive oil

1½ lb chicken thighs on the bone

2 onions, minced

⅓ teaspoon ground cinnamon

A pinch of saffron threads

1 teaspoon ground ginger

1 bunch of cilantro, leaves chopped

⅔ cup water, plus extra as required

Salt and freshly ground black pepper

2 tablespoons toasted sesame seeds, to garnish

For the caramelized apples:

3 Braeburn apples, peeled, cored, and thickly sliced

2 teaspoons honey

2 tablespoons butter

1 small cinnamon stick

¼ teaspoon nutmeg

For the caramelized apples, place the apples, honey, butter, cinnamon stick, and nutmeg in the bottom of the tagine and cook over low heat until the apples begin to caramelize. Remove from the tagine and set aside.

Wipe the bottom of the tagine, then add the oil. Heat over medium heat, add the chicken thighs, and brown them on all sides. Remove with a slotted spoon and set aside.

Add the onions and fry for 3 to 4 minutes until softened. Stir in the ground cinnamon, saffron, ginger, and cilantro leaves. Return the chicken to the bottom of the tagine, season with salt and pepper, pour in the measured water, and stir well.

Bring to a boil, then reduce the heat to very low, cover with the lid, and cook the chicken for 1½ hours until cooked through. Check occasionally that there is enough moisture in the tagine and, if necessary, add extra water as required.

Add the caramelized apples to the tagine and serve scattered with sesame seeds.

Cast Iron Rectangular Grill

STUFFED HERB CHICKEN WITH CHERRY TOMATOES

Crispy griddled chicken with a delicious surprise inside.

SERVES 6
Preparation time: 15 minutes
Cooking time: 25 minutes

6 chicken thighs

⅓ cup mascarpone cheese

3 tablespoons olive oil

1 lb 2 oz cherry tomatoes

For the herb sauce:

3 tablespoons olive oil

2 garlic cloves, minced

4 canned anchovy fillets, drained and finely chopped

2 tablespoons capers, drained and finely chopped

1 tablespoon wholegrain mustard

1 handful of tarragon leaves, chopped

1 handful of basil leaves, chopped

1 handful of flat-leaf parsley leaves, chopped

2 tablespoons lemon juice

Salt and freshly ground black pepper

Mix together all the ingredients for the herb sauce, and season with salt and pepper.

Using a sharp knife, make a cut in the thickest part of each chicken thigh to make a pocket.

Mix ¼ cup of the herb sauce with the mascarpone and spoon 1 tablespoon of the mixture into each pocket. Close the opening and secure with a toothpick.

Brush the chicken with the oil and season with salt and pepper. Heat the skillet grill over high heat and grease with a little oil. Place half of the chicken in the pan and chargrill for 5 minutes at a high temperature. Reduce the temperature and cook for another 10 minutes, covered. Carefully adjust the chicken thighs with a spatula so that they brown evenly. Turn the chicken over and chargrill the other side for 10 minutes until golden brown and cooked through. Remove from the skillet grill, cover, and keep warm in a low oven while you cook the remaining chicken.

Add the cherry tomatoes to the skillet grill 5 minutes before the end of the cooking time and cook until softened.

Serve the chicken with the cherry tomatoes and any remaining herb sauce.

CHICKEN WITH OLIVES & PRESERVED LEMON

A classic tagine of slow-cooked chicken with olives, preserved lemons, and spices.

2-quart Tagine

SERVES 4
Preparation time: 20 minutes
Cooking time: 1½ hours

1 tablespoon olive oil

2¼ lb whole chicken, cut into 8 pieces

2 onions, minced

2 garlic cloves, minced

2 tablespoons lemon juice

1 bunch of cilantro, leaves chopped, divided

1 teaspoon ground ginger

1 teaspoon ground cumin

A pinch of saffron threads

1 small cinnamon stick

1 cup water or light chicken stock, plus extra as required

2 small preserved lemons, seeds removed and the skin cut into fine strips

¾ cup black or green olives, pitted

Salt and freshly ground black pepper

Heat the oil in the bottom of the tagine over medium heat, add the chicken pieces, and brown on all sides. Remove with a slotted spoon and set aside.

Add the onions and garlic and fry for 5 to 6 minutes until soft. Return the chicken to the tagine.

Stir in the lemon juice, half the cilantro leaves, ginger, cumin, saffron, cinnamon stick, and the measured water or stock. Reduce the heat to very low, cover with the lid, and cook the chicken for 1½ hours until cooked through. Check occasionally that there is enough moisture in the tagine and, if necessary, add extra water or stock as required.

Rinse the preserved lemons and olives under cold running water to remove any excess salt and stir them into the tagine. Replace the lid and cook for a further 10 minutes.

Season the tagine with salt and pepper and scatter with the remaining cilantro to serve.

NOTE: *Ask your butcher to cut up the chicken for you.*

BELGIAN CHICKEN PIE WITH LIME & TARRAGON PESTO

A puff pastry crust is the perfect finishing touch for this creamy pie.

2-quart Round Dutch Oven

SERVES 4
Preparation time: 25 minutes
Cooking time: 50 minutes

For the lime and tarragon pesto:

½ cup tarragon leaves

2 garlic cloves, peeled and left whole

3 tablespoons toasted pine nuts

½ cup pecorino cheese, grated

Juice of 1 lime

⅔ cup olive oil

Salt and freshly ground black pepper

For the stock:

2¼ lb chicken

2 quarts water

2 leeks, green part left whole,
white part thinly sliced

3 celery stalks, 1 left whole,
2 stalks cut into small pieces

1 onion

3 thyme sprigs

1 bay leaf

For the pie:

1½ tablespoons butter

⅓ cup all-purpose flour, plus extra
for rolling

4 to 6 large round red or round white
potatoes, peeled, cut into 1-inch dice,
and parboiled for 8 minutes

2 carrots, thinly sliced

½ fennel bulb, thinly sliced

1¼ cups heavy cream

A pinch of cayenne pepper

9 oz ready-made puff pastry

1 egg, lightly beaten

For the pesto, add the tarragon, garlic, pine nuts, pecorino, and lime juice to a blender and process until finely chopped. While blending, slowly drizzle in enough of the oil to make a smooth paste and season with salt and pepper.

For the stock, place the chicken in the Dutch oven, add the measured water, the green part of the leeks, 1 whole celery stalk, the onion, thyme, and bay leaf. Season well with salt and pepper. Bring to a boil, then reduce the heat to medium, cover with the lid, and simmer for 30 minutes.

Turn off the heat and let the chicken cool down in the stock. When cooled, lift the chicken from the stock, remove the skin, and remove the cooked chicken from the carcass in large pieces. Strain the stock through a sieve and reserve.

Melt the butter in the Dutch oven over medium-low heat, add the flour, and cook for 2 minutes, stirring. Stir in half of the strained stock and bring to a boil, stirring, until thickened. Continue to add the stock until the consistency of a thick cream soup.

Preheat the oven to 425°F. Stir the carrots, fennel, white part of the leeks, chopped celery, parboiled potatoes, and cream into the sauce. Return the cooked chicken pieces to the Dutch oven and season with cayenne pepper.

Lightly dust a work surface with flour and roll out the pastry into a circle large enough to cover the top of the Dutch oven with a little overhang. Place the pastry over the top of the Dutch oven, press the edges down, and trim off any excess. Brush the pastry top with the beaten egg and bake for 10 to 15 minutes until the pastry is golden and well risen.

Serve the chicken pie with the pesto.

2-quart Tagine

CHICKEN WITH ROOT VEGETABLES

The root vegetables add color and flavor to this simple chicken tagine.

SERVES 4
Preparation time: 10 minutes
Cooking time: 1 hour 50 minutes

1 tablespoon olive oil

2 shallots, chopped

1 garlic clove, chopped

1½ lb chicken thighs on the bone

1 teaspoon mild paprika

1 bay leaf

1 oregano sprig

1 rosemary sprig

2 tablespoons lemon juice

1 cup water, plus extra as required

1 lb 2 oz mixed root vegetables, such as Jerusalem artichokes, purple carrots, rutabaga, baby turnips, and parsnips, cut into equal-sized pieces

Salt and freshly ground black pepper

½ bunch of flat-leaf parsley, leaves chopped, to garnish

Heat the oil in the bottom of the tagine over medium heat, add the shallots and garlic, and fry for 4 to 5 minutes until lightly caramelized.

Add the chicken thighs and sauté for 10 minutes, turning occasionally, until browned on all sides.

Stir in the paprika, bay leaf, oregano, rosemary, lemon juice, and the measured water. Season with salt and pepper. Reduce the heat to very low, cover with the lid, and cook the chicken for 1 hour.

After 1 hour, spread the root vegetables over the chicken in the tagine and mix everything well. Replace the lid and cook for a further 50 minutes, or until the vegetables are tender. Check occasionally that there is enough moisture in the tagine and, if necessary, add extra water or stock as required.

Scatter with the parsley before serving.

Cast Iron Rectangular
Skinny Grill

SERVES 6
Preparation time: 20 minutes
Cooking time: 15 minutes

6 skinless, boneless turkey
fillets, about 5½ oz each

For the herb crust:

10 sage leaves

4 thyme sprigs, leaves only

4 flat-leaf parsley sprigs, leaves only

1 tablespoon dried basil

⅓ cup olive oil, plus extra for brushing

3 tablespoons lemon juice

½ cup pine nuts

½ cup bread crumbs

½ cup grated Parmesan cheese

HERB-CRUSTED TURKEY BROCHETTES

The herb, Parmesan, and pine nut coating gives the turkey skewers a flavor boost and a crisp golden crust.

For the herb crust, blend together the fresh and dried herbs with the oil, lemon juice, and pine nuts to form a green sauce. Spoon the sauce into a bowl and stir in the bread crumbs and Parmesan.

Add the turkey to the green sauce, then roll it in the sauce to coat. Thread the turkey onto skewers. (If you are using wooden skewers, soak them for an hour in water before use to prevent them from charring or burning.)

Heat the skillet grill over medium-high heat and brush with oil. Cook the turkey brochettes for 10 to 15 minutes, or until browned and cooked through, turning once. (Be careful when turning them over.)

Why not serve the brochettes with baked potatoes, salad, and a spoonful of sour cream?

5-quart Oval Dutch Oven

Serves 6
Preparation time: 15 minutes
Cooking time: 1 hour 10 minutes

TURKEY & APRICOTS IN ALE

Ale, rosemary, and apricots add plenty of flavor to this rich turkey stew.

2¼ lb skinless, boneless turkey thigh meat, cut into 1-inch cubes

2 tablespoons butter

2 tablespoons vegetable oil

3 cups halved, pitted fresh apricots (or 8 to 9 dried apricots, cut in half, soaked in 1 cup water for 1 hour and drained)

2 cups light ale or Belgian beer, such as Gueuze

1 red onion, thinly sliced

2 garlic cloves, crushed

3 rosemary sprigs, divided

½ cup chicken stock

Salt and freshly ground black pepper

Season the turkey with salt and pepper.

Heat the butter and oil in the Dutch oven over medium heat, add half of the turkey, and cook until browned on all sides. Remove with a slotted spoon and repeat with the remaining turkey, then set aside.

Finely chop 4 of the apricots and add to the Dutch oven with the browned turkey, light ale or beer, onion, garlic, 1 rosemary sprig, and the stock. Bring to a simmer, reduce the heat to low, and cook for 1 hour, stirring occasionally.

Pour the cooking sauce into a pitcher, retaining the solids in the Dutch oven, and remove the rosemary sprig and any loose leaves. Strain the cooking sauce to remove any lumps and pour it back into the Dutch oven along with the retained solids.

Add the remaining rosemary to the Dutch oven with the rest of the apricots. Adjust the seasoning, to taste, then heat through until the apricots are tender, and serve.

GUINEA FOWL WITH PEARS & HARD CIDER

A dish that captures the rich, traditional taste of Normandy.

14½ x 12½-inch Rectangular
Cast Iron Dish

SERVES 4
Preparation time: 15 minutes
Cooking time: 50 minutes

2 guinea fowl, cut into pieces

1½ tablespoons butter

3 tablespoons Calvados

4 shallots, minced

3 bay leaves

2 cups hard cider

½ cup chicken stock

6 pears, peeled and left whole

1 vanilla bean, split lengthwise

1 tablespoon heavy cream

2 tablespoons cornstarch

Salt and freshly ground black pepper

Season the guinea fowl with salt and pepper.

Preheat the oven to 325°F.

Heat the butter in the cast iron dish over medium heat, add the guinea fowl, and brown on all sides. Pour in the Calvados and cook until reduced.

Add the shallots and bay leaves and pour in the hard cider and chicken stock.

Arrange the pears in the dish and add the vanilla bean.

Cover with foil and roast the guinea fowl in the oven for 20 minutes. Remove the foil, add the cream, and return the dish to the oven for another 15 minutes until the guinea fowl is cooked. If the sauce needs thickening, stir in the cornstarch and cook for another 5 minutes. Remove the vanilla bean before serving.

HERB-STUFFED PIGEON WITH GRAPES

The gaminess of the pigeon works perfectly with the bacon and grapes in this casserole.

4½-quart Round Dutch Oven

SERVES 6
Preparation time: 20 minutes
Cooking time: 1 hour 10 minutes

6 oven-ready wood pigeons

1 bunch of flat-leaf parsley, chopped

1 bunch of tarragon, chopped

12 thin slices of bacon, divided

½ stick butter, divided

1 tablespoon olive oil, plus extra
if needed

1 sweet white onion, chopped

2 garlic cloves, crushed

3 celery stalks, finely diced

1 tablespoon all-purpose flour

1¼ cups Muscat wine

2½ cups chicken stock

2 tablespoons wholegrain mustard

1 lb 2 oz seedless red and seedless
green grapes

Salt and freshly ground black pepper

Preheat the oven to 325°F.

Season the pigeons with salt and pepper. Stuff the pigeons with the parsley and half of the tarragon. Wrap 2 slices of bacon around each pigeon.

Heat 1 tablespoon of the butter and the olive oil in the Dutch oven over medium heat, add three of the pigeons, and brown them on all sides. Remove them from the Dutch oven and repeat with the remaining pigeons, adding more oil, if necessary.

Add the onion, garlic, and celery to the Dutch oven and fry until soft. Add the remaining butter. When it has melted, stir in the flour. Pour in the wine, stir, and cook gently until reduced by half.

Return the pigeons to the Dutch oven and add the stock and wholegrain mustard. Cover with the lid and transfer to the oven to cook for 40 minutes.

Add the grapes and the remaining tarragon, cover, and return to the oven for a further 10 minutes. Season with salt and pepper before serving.

2-quart Tagine

SERVES 4
Preparation time: 15 minutes
Cooking time: 1 hour 10 minutes

BRAISED QUAILS WITH MEDJOOL DATES

Quails in an aromatic sauce with sticky dates and finished with toasted sesame seeds.

2 tablespoons olive oil, divided

4 oven-ready quails

2 small onions, minced

⅔ cup water or light chicken stock

1 small cinnamon stick

A pinch of saffron threads

⅓ teaspoon ground ginger

½ lb Medjool dates, pitted and cut in half

2 teaspoons butter

2 teaspoons honey

Salt and freshly ground black pepper

2 tablespoons sesame seeds (optional), to garnish

Heat 1 tablespoon of the oil in the bottom of the tagine over medium heat, add two of the quails, and brown them on all sides. Remove the quails and set aside while you cook the two remaining quails, adding more oil if necessary. Set all the quails aside.

Add the remaining oil and fry the onions, stirring occasionally, until lightly caramelized.

Add the measured water or stock to the tagine along with the cinnamon stick, saffron, and ginger and season with salt and pepper. Bring the sauce to a boil and return the quails to the tagine.

Reduce the heat to very low, cover with the lid, and cook for 40 minutes.

Stir the dates, butter, and honey into the tagine. Replace the lid and cook for a further 15 minutes until the quails are done. Adjust the seasoning to taste with salt and pepper, and serve scattered with sesame seeds, if you like.

DUCK LEGS WITH BEETS & CARAWAY

A rich and comforting combination of duck and root vegetables.

2-quart Tagine

SERVES 2
Preparation time: 20 minutes
Cooking time: 2¾ hours

2 duck legs

2 small onions, minced

1 garlic clove, chopped

1 bouquet garni

½ teaspoon caraway seeds

½ cup red wine

½ chicken stock cube

¾ lb uncooked beets, cut into quarters and thickly sliced

2 carrots, thickly sliced

Salt and freshly ground black pepper

1 bunch of flat-leaf parsley, leaves chopped, to garnish

Using the tip of a sharp knife, make diagonal cuts into the skin of each duck leg.

Put the duck legs, skin-side down, in the bottom of the tagine and cook over low heat for 10 minutes until the fat starts to run and the skin is golden.

Add the onions and garlic to the duck, increase the heat to medium, and fry for 5 minutes until soft.

Pour off any excess oil, then add the bouquet garni, caraway seeds, and red wine. Crumble in the stock cube and season with salt and pepper. Reduce the heat to low, cover with the lid, and cook the duck legs for 2 hours, or until tender. Check occasionally that there is enough moisture in the tagine and, if necessary, add some water as required.

Add the beets and carrots to the tagine. Replace the lid and cook for a further 30 minutes over low heat, or until the vegetables are tender. Scatter with parsley before serving.

8-inch Square Stoneware Dish

SERVES 4
Preparation time: 20 minutes
Cooking time: 1¼ hours

DUCK WITH GLAZED TURNIPS
Duck and ale are an unusual combination but they work together beautifully in this dish.

2 tablespoons butter

4 duck breasts

4 rosemary sprigs, leaves removed in small sprigs

8 small turnips, cut into quarters

12 small round red or round white potatoes, cut into small, evenly sized pieces

1 tablespoon brown sugar

1 bottle dark ale, about 12 fl oz

½ cup chicken stock

1 teaspoon cornstarch

Salt and freshly ground black pepper

Preheat the oven to 325°F.

Put the butter in the stoneware dish and heat it in the oven until melted.

Using the tip of a sharp knife, make diagonal cuts into the skin of each duck leg. Insert the rosemary sprigs in the gaps between the skin and the meat and season with salt and pepper.

Arrange the duck breasts in the butter-coated dish, cover with foil, and cook in the oven for 45 minutes.

Remove the dish from the oven and pour off any excess fat. Add the turnips and potatoes, sprinkle with the sugar, and season with salt and pepper.

Turn the oven down to 315°F. Pour the ale and stock into the dish, stir, and return it to the oven for 30 minutes, or until the vegetables are tender.

Remove the dish from the oven and thicken the sauce with the cornstarch, if needed. Adjust the seasoning, to taste, and serve in the dish.

Round Skillet Grill

DUCK, PRUNE & ORANGE BROCHETTES

A modern twist on duck à l'orange, the French classic.

SERVES 6 ·
Preparation time: 20 minutes, plus marinating
Cooking time: 10 minutes

---

12 dried prunes, pitted and cut in half

2 tablespoons Armagnac

4 rosemary sprigs, leaves picked and finely chopped

2 tablespoons pink peppercorns

½ teaspoon fine sea salt

3 duck boneless breasts, about 7 oz each, fat removed, cut into
1-inch cubes

1 large orange, cut into bite-sized pieces

A few bay leaves

Juice of ½ orange

Olive oil, for brushing

Soak the prunes in the Armagnac for 30 minutes until softened, then drain, discarding any remaining Armagnac.

Crush the rosemary leaves with the pink peppercorns and salt in a mortar and pestle. Rub the duck cubes in half of the rosemary mixture.

Thread the duck onto skewers, interspersed with pieces of orange, bay leaves, and prune. Repeat to make 6 skewers in total. (If you are using wooden skewers, soak them for an hour in water before use to prevent them from charring or burning.)

Squeeze a little orange juice over the skewers, brush them with oil, and sprinkle with the rest of the rosemary mixture.

Heat the skillet grill over high heat and lightly brush with oil. Put the brochettes in the skillet grill and chargrill, turning them occasionally so they do not burn, until the duck is cooked and starting to color.

Square Skillet Grill

RABBIT BROCHETTES WITH SAGE & LEMON

Perfect for lunch on a hot summer's day.

SERVES 6

Preparation time: 15 minutes, plus marinating
Cooking time: 15 minutes

1 lb 10 oz rabbit fillets

3 zucchini, sliced into ribbons

Oil, for brushing

For the marinade:

Peel and juice of 1 lemon

2 garlic cloves

2 sage sprigs, leaves removed

½ cup olive oil

Salt and freshly ground pepper

For the marinade, blanch the lemon peel in boiling water for 2 minutes, then rinse immediately in cold water. Finely chop the lemon peel, garlic, and sage leaves. Add the olive oil and season with salt and pepper.

Place the rabbit pieces in one bowl and the zucchini ribbons in another. Divide the marinade between the bowls, stir, and let marinate for 2 hours.

Thread the rabbit fillets onto skewers. (If you are using wooden skewers, soak them for an hour in water before use to prevent them from charring or burning.) Set aside.

Heat the skillet grill over high heat and lightly brush with oil. Chargrill the zucchini ribbons for 5 minutes, or until blackened in places. Remove and set aside.

Cook the duck brochettes for 5 to 6 minutes on each side. Serve the rabbit brochettes with the zucchini and add a squeeze of lemon juice before serving.

2- or 4½-quart Round Dutch Oven

RABBIT IN GORGONZOLA SAUCE

A surprising and delicious combination of rabbit and pears in a creamy cheese sauce.

SERVES 4

Preparation time: 20 minutes
Cooking time: 1¼ hours

1 prepared rabbit, cut into pieces

2 tablespoons butter

1 tablespoon olive oil

2 garlic cloves, sliced

1 sage sprig, leaves sliced,
plus extra to garnish

½ cup white port

2 cups chicken stock

1¾ cups heavy cream

7 oz Gorgonzola cheese, crumbled

2 pears, peeled, cored,
and cut into wedges

Salt and freshly ground black pepper

Season the rabbit with salt and pepper.

Melt the butter and oil in the Dutch oven over medium heat, add the rabbit, and cook for 10 minutes until browned on all sides. Stir in the garlic and sage.

Pour in the port and cook, stirring to release any brown bits sticking to the bottom, until reduced. Add the chicken stock and bring to a boil. Cover with the lid, reduce the heat to low, and simmer for 1 hour, turning the rabbit occasionally.

Remove the rabbit from the Dutch oven with a slotted spoon and keep it warm. Bring the sauce in the casserole to a boil, stir in the cream, and cook until reduced and thickened.

Stir the Gorgonzola into the sauce and season with salt and pepper.

Add the pears and return the warm rabbit pieces to the Dutch oven. Heat through to piping hot and serve garnished with the extra sage.

NOTE: *Ask your butcher to prepare the rabbit for you.*

FISH & SEAFOOD

SOUTH AFRICAN SEAFOOD STEW (POTJIEKOS)

An authentic fish and shellfish stew that packs a powerful punch.

2- or 4½-quart Round Dutch Oven

SERVES 4
Preparation time: 20 minutes, plus marinating
Cooking time: 35 minutes

For the piri piri marinade:

Juice of 2 lemons

2 tablespoons vegetable oil, divided

1 tablespoon chopped cilantro

2 to 4 fresh chiles, seeded and chopped

2 garlic cloves, peeled

For the seafood stew:

1 lb 2 oz firm white fish fillets, such as bream, bass, monkfish or gurnard, skinned and cut into pieces

1 tablespoon butter

2 red onions, cut into quarters

3 potatoes, cut into wedges

2 tomatoes, cut into quarters

1¾ cups fish stock, plus extra if required

1 teaspoon ground ginger

8 dried apricots

3½ oz raw jumbo shrimp, head and vein removed

3½ oz cooked mussels in their shell

A few cilantro sprigs, to garnish

For the piri piri marinade, put the lemon juice, 1 tablespoon of the oil, cilantro, chiles, and garlic in a mini food processor and pulse to a paste.

Put the white fish in a nonmetallic dish, add the marinade, and gently roll the fish in the marinade until coated. Cover and let marinate in the refrigerator for at least 30 minutes.

Heat the remaining oil and the butter in the Dutch oven over medium heat, add the onions and potatoes, and fry for 5 minutes, or until the onions are soft.

Add the tomatoes, fish stock, ginger, and apricots. Bring to a simmer and cook for 15 minutes.

Add the marinated fish to the sauce. Check that there is enough sauce and add extra stock, if needed. Simmer the fish for 10 minutes, then add the shrimp and cook for a further 5 minutes until pink. A couple of minutes before the shrimp are cooked, stir in the mussels and heat through. Garnish with cilantro sprigs before serving.

**Cast Iron Rectangular
Skinny Grill**

SERVES 6
Preparation time: 15 minutes
Cooking time: 10 minutes

GRIDDLED FISH WITH TOMATOES & OLIVES

**Light and summery, this simple fish dish captures
the flavors of the Mediterranean.**

6 whole fish, such as trout or whiting,
gutted and cleaned

1 teaspoon dried oregano

1 teaspoon dried thyme

3 lemons, cut in half and sliced

⅓ cup lemon oil, divided

1 lb 2 oz cherry tomatoes, cut in half

½ cup green olives

A few flat-leaf parsley sprigs,
leaves chopped

Salt and freshly ground black pepper

Heat the nonstick griddle over high heat.

Score the skin of each fish on both sides. Season with the oregano, thyme, salt, and pepper and fill the cavity of the fish with some of the lemon slices.

Brush the hot griddle with some of the lemon oil. Arrange the fish in the griddle and scatter with the remaining lemon slices. Cook the fish for 3 to 4 minutes on each side until the skin is crisp and golden and the fish just cooked through. Turn the fish carefully so you do not damage the skin.

Mix the tomatoes with the olives and parsley. Drizzle with a little of the lemon oil and season with salt and pepper. Serve the fish, drizzled with any juices left behind in the pan, with the tomato, olives, and parsley, and some crusty bread.

PISTACHIO-CRUSTED COD WITH TOMATOES & CAPERS

Fish fillets topped with a nutty crust and cooked with a cherry tomato and caper sauce.

2-quart Tagine

SERVES 4
Preparation time: 15 minutes
Cooking time: 50 minutes

¼ cup olive oil, divided

5 shallots, minced

2 garlic cloves, minced

A pinch of mild paprika

2 tablespoons salted capers, rinsed and drained

2 bay leaves

1½ lb cherry tomatoes

1 lb 2 oz cod fillet, skinned, boned, and cut into 4 pieces

Salt and freshly ground black pepper

For the pistachio crust:

2 tablespoons shelled unsalted pistachios, chopped

½ bunch of flat-leaf parsley, leaves chopped

½ bunch of cilantro, leaves chopped

5 chives, snipped

Heat 2 tablespoons of the oil in the bottom of the tagine over medium heat, add the shallots and garlic, and fry for 1 minute. Mix in the paprika and fry for a further 4 to 5 minutes, stirring occasionally, until the shallots are soft.

Add the capers, bay leaves, and tomatoes. Season with a pinch of salt and stir everything together. Reduce the heat to low, cover with the lid, and cook for 30 minutes. Check occasionally to see if there is enough moisture in the tagine and, if needed, add some water as required.

For the pistachio crust, mix the pistachios, parsley, cilantro, and chives in a bowl with the remaining 2 tablespoons of oil and season with salt and pepper.

Spread the pistachio crust over the pieces of fish and place them in the tagine on top of the tomato mixture. Replace the lid and cook for 10 to 15 minutes, depending on the thickness of the fish. Serve immediately.

4½-quart Round Dutch Oven

COD & POTATO CASSEROLE

A light and healthy fish casserole with a hint of orange.

SERVES 4
Preparation time: 10 minutes
Cooking time: 45 minutes

3 tablespoons olive oil

1 red onion, sliced

10½ oz potatoes, scrubbed and sliced

1 leek, sliced

3 tablespoons dry white wine

⅔ cup fish stock

1½ medium zucchini, sliced

14 oz cod steaks, boned
and cut into 2 pieces

2 to 3 dill sprigs

½ cup milk

2 scallions, chopped

Zest and juice of ½ orange

Salt and freshly ground black pepper

Heat the oil in the Dutch oven over medium heat, add the onion and potatoes, and fry for 5 minutes until the onion is soft. Add the leek and mix well.

Pour in the wine, bring to a boil, and cook until it is reduced by half. Add the stock, cover with the lid, and reduce the heat to low. Cook gently for 20 minutes until the potatoes are almost tender.

Add the zucchini, cod, and dill to the Dutch oven. Cover with the lid and cook for a further 15 minutes until the cod is cooked and flakes apart easily.

Stir in the milk, season with salt and pepper, and heat through.

Stir in the scallions and the orange zest and juice and serve.

2-quart Tagine

SERVES 3
Preparation time: 15 minutes
Cooking time: 1 hour

CITRUS, CHILE & CILANTRO-MARINATED SWORDFISH

Swordfish steaks in a feisty citrus marinade cooked with spiced new potatoes.

10½ oz new potatoes, scrubbed and sliced

½ teaspoon ground cumin

½ teaspoon ground coriander

3 bay leaves

⅔ cup water, plus extra as required

3 swordfish steaks

½ lemon, cut in half

Salt and freshly ground black pepper

For the marinade:

3 garlic cloves, chopped

1 bunch of cilantro, leaves chopped

1 small red chile, seeded and cut into fine strips

Juice of 2 lemons

2 tablespoons olive oil

Place the potato slices in the bottom of the tagine, stir in the cumin, coriander, and bay leaves, add the measured water, and season with salt and pepper. Cover with the lid and cook the potatoes over low heat for 40 minutes, or until almost tender. Check occasionally to see if there is enough moisture in the tagine and, if needed, add extra water as required.

Meanwhile make the marinade. Mix together the garlic, cilantro leaves, chile, lemon juice, and oil in a large, shallow dish. Place the swordfish steaks in a nonmetallic dish and gently roll them in the marinade to coat. Cover and let marinate in the refrigerator for 30 minutes.

Remove the dish from the fridge, take the fish out of the marinade, and place it on top of the potatoes. Drizzle the fish with the marinade, replace the lid, and cook for a further 15 to 20 minutes, or until the fish is just cooked and the potatoes are tender. Sprinkle with a squeeze of fresh lemon juice from the remaining lemon half, to taste, just before serving.

Square Skillet Grill

SERVES 6
Preparation time: 30 minutes, plus marinating
Cooking time: 10 minutes

SWORDFISH, CHORIZO & SUN-DRIED TOMATO BROCHETTES

The fish is flavored with smoky chorizo, basil, and rich sun-dried tomatoes—perfect for a light summery meal.

1 lb 5 oz swordfish or monkfish, membrane removed, cut into 1-inch cubes

12 thick slices of chorizo

12 basil leaves

12 sun-dried tomatoes in oil, drained

1 teaspoon paprika

Salt and freshly ground black pepper

For the marinade:

½ cup olive oil

3 tablespoons balsamic vinegar

1 tablespoon port

Thread a piece of fish, a slice of chorizo, a basil leaf, and a sun-dried tomato on a brochette stick, then repeat so each skewer has two of each. Make 6 skewers in total, then season with pepper and the paprika. (If you are using wooden skewers, soak them for an hour in water before use to prevent them from charring or burning.)

Mix together all the ingredients for the marinade in a shallow nonmetallic dish. Season with salt and pepper. Place the brochettes in the dish and drizzle with the marinade to coat. Let stand to marinate in the dish for at least 15 minutes, or until ready to cook.

Heat the skillet grill over high heat. Add the brochettes, drizzle with some of the marinade, and cook for 5 minutes on each side, or until the fish is cooked through.

Serve the brochettes with a crisp salad.

2-quart Tagine

SERVES 4
Preparation time: 20 minutes
Cooking time: 1 hour 10 minutes

MONKFISH WITH OLIVES & NEW POTATOES

Meaty fish in a spicy sauce with green olives, new potatoes, and preserved lemon.

1 tablespoon olive oil

1 garlic clove, chopped

1 small red bell pepper, seeded and sliced

½ cup dry white wine

1 bunch of cilantro, tied together with kitchen string

1 teaspoon ground cumin

1 teaspoon mild paprika

1 teaspoon hot paprika

½ teaspoon ground turmeric

10½ oz new potatoes, cut in half lengthwise

⅔ cup water, plus extra as required

1 preserved lemon, rinsed, pulp and seeds discarded, skin cut into small dice

1 cup green olives, rinsed and pitted

1½ lb skinned, boned monkfish, membrane removed, cut into 8 pieces

Salt and freshly ground black pepper

Heat the oil in the bottom of the tagine over low heat, add the garlic and red bell pepper, and fry for 10 minutes, stirring regularly, until soft. Increase the heat to medium, pour in the white wine, and cook for 5 minutes until reduced.

Add the bunch of cilantro, cumin, mild and hot paprika, turmeric, potatoes, the measured water, and a little salt.

Reduce the heat to low, cover with the lid, and cook for 40 minutes, or until the potatoes are nearly cooked. Check occasionally to see if there is enough moisture in the tagine and, if needed, add some extra water as required.

Add the preserved lemon, olives, and the monkfish pieces to the tagine and gently stir to combine. Replace the lid and cook for a further 15 minutes, or until the fish is just cooked. Remove the cilantro bunch and season the fish to taste before serving.

5-quart Oval Dutch Oven

SERVES 4
Preparation time: 20 minutes
Cooking time: 15 minutes

2 sea bream, about ¾ lb each,
gutted and cleaned

4 limes, peeled, divided

8 dill sprigs

6 mint sprigs

6 tarragon sprigs

2 pink pomelos or 1 pink grapefruit,
peeled

2 oranges, peeled

2 lemons, peeled

1 tablespoon olive oil

1 tablespoon butter

2 garlic cloves, sliced

2 shallots, sliced

1 red chile, seeded and finely chopped

4 bay leaves

1¾ cups fish stock

Salt and freshly ground black pepper

SEA BREAM WITH CITRUS
Fish cooked in a delicious combination of citrus fruits and fresh herbs.

Season the fish inside and out with salt and pepper. Cut three of the limes into thin wedges. Stuff the bream with the sprigs of dill, mint, tarragon, and lime wedges.

Cut the pomelos or grapefruit, oranges, lemons, and the remaining lime into segments, cutting between the white membranes with a small sharp knife. Do this over a bowl to catch any juices and reserve.

Heat the oil and butter in the Dutch oven over medium heat, add the garlic, shallots, chile, and bay leaves and fry for 1 to 2 minutes until softened. Add the stuffed fish, the citrus fruit, and any reserved juices and cook for 3 minutes.

Add the stock to the fish, cover with the lid, and cook over low heat for 5 to 10 minutes, or until the fish is cooked through. The cooking time will depend on the thickness of the fish.

The bream is delicious served with new potatoes.

14½ x 12½-inch Rectangular Stoneware Dish

SERVES 4
Preparation time: 15 minutes
Cooking time: 30 minutes

BAKED SEA BASS IN SALT CRUST

The salt crust keeps the fish moist and flavorsome while it bakes.

2 sea bass

2 rosemary sprigs

2 thyme sprigs

2 sage sprigs

1 lime, peeled and cut into thin wedges, plus extra to serve

2¼ lb coarse sea salt

2 egg whites

For the tomato and almond sauce:

1 shallot, peeled

1 tomato

1 egg

1 teaspoon mustard

1 tablespoon red wine vinegar

3 tablespoon olive oil

¼ cup ground almonds

Salt and freshly ground black pepper

Preheat the oven to 350°F.

Season the sea bass with pepper. Stuff the fish with the herb sprigs and lime wedges.

Mix the sea salt and egg whites into a paste. Spoon a thin layer of the paste in the stoneware dish. Place the sea bass on top and cover completely with the remaining paste. Bake for 30 minutes.

Meanwhile, make the tomato and almond sauce. Add the shallot, tomato, egg, mustard, and vinegar to a blender. Blend until combined, then gradually pour in the oil. Add the ground almonds, season with salt and pepper, and blend until smooth and creamy.

To serve, break open the salt crust surrounding the sea bass. Fillet the fish using a spoon and fork and arrange on serving plates. Serve with the tomato and almond sauce on the side, along with extra wedges of lime.

2-quart Tagine

SERVES 4
Preparation time: 15 minutes
Cooking time: 1 hour 5 minutes

SEA BASS WITH CHERRY TOMATOES, LEMON & POTATOES

A light, summery white fish tagine in a lemon sauce with cherry tomatoes and new potatoes.

2¼ lb small new potatoes, scrubbed or peeled and cut in half

1 garlic clove, chopped

1 bunch of cilantro, leaves chopped

Juice of 2 lemons

4 bay leaves

½ teaspoon ground coriander

¼ teaspoon hot chili powder

3 tablespoons olive oil, divided

10½ oz yellow and red cherry tomatoes, cut in half if large

½ cup water, plus extra as required

1¼ lb skinned and boned sea bass, cut into 4 pieces

Salt and freshly ground black pepper

1 teaspoon fennel seeds, to garnish

Place the potatoes, garlic, cilantro leaves, lemon juice, bay leaves, ground coriander, chili powder, 2 tablespoons of the oil, and the cherry tomatoes in the tagine. Season with salt and pepper and add the measured water.

Cover with the lid and cook over very low heat for 50 minutes. Check occasionally that the vegetables are not sticking to the bottom of the tagine and add extra water as required.

Place the sea bass on top of the vegetables, season with a little salt and pepper, and drizzle with the remaining oil. Cover and continue to cook for 10 to 15 minutes until the fish is just done. The cooking time will depend on the thickness of the fish.

Sprinkle with the fennel seeds before serving.

NOTE: *This recipe also works well with monkfish or halibut.*

Square Skillet Grill

SALMON FILLETS WITH ASIAN SALAD

The Asian dressing in this recipe is a combination of salty, sweet, and sour—delicious with the bean sprout salad and salmon.

SERVES 6
Preparation time: 10 minutes
Cooking time: 10 minutes

1 cup bean sprouts

2 tablespoons toasted sesame seeds

Coconut oil, for cooking

6 salmon fillets, about 7 oz each

A few dill sprigs, to garnish

For the dressing:

Finely grated zest and juice of 2 limes

2 tablespoons plum sauce

2 tablespoons rice vinegar

1 tablespoon sesame oil

1 tablespoon light soy sauce

Salt and freshly ground black pepper

For the dressing, mix together all the ingredients and season with a little salt and pepper.

Mix the bean sprouts with 1 tablespoon of the sesame seeds and drizzle with a few tablespoons of the dressing. Set aside.

Heat the skillet grill over high heat. Lightly oil the pan with the coconut oil and grill the salmon, skin-side down first, for 2 to 3 minutes until the skin is crisp. Carefully turn the salmon over and cook the other side until almost cooked through, but still slightly pink in the middle.

Remove the salmon from the pan and let rest for a few minutes. Season the fish with salt and pepper and garnish with a few sprigs of dill.

Serve with the bean sprout salad and extra dressing on the side.

1-quart Cast Iron Oval Au Gratin

BAKED HADDOCK WITH LEMON BUTTER SAUCE

Haddock cooked simply in a lemony butter sauce—what could be better?

SERVES 4
Preparation time: 10 minutes
Cooking time: 15 minutes

4 thick haddock fillets

½ stick butter

4 shallots, thinly sliced

2 lemons, cut in half

¼ bunch of flat-leaf parsley, leaves chopped

Salt and freshly ground black pepper

Preheat the oven to 350°F.

Score the skin of each haddock or cod fillet with a sharp knife, to prevent it from curling during cooking. Season the fillets with salt and pepper.

Heat the butter in the cast iron au gratin in the oven until melted and starting to brown.

Arrange the fish in the dish, spoon the melted butter evenly over it, and cook in the oven for 5 minutes.

Scatter with the shallots, drizzle with any juices in the bottom of the dish, and return it to the oven for another 5 to 10 minutes until the haddock is just cooked and the shallots have softened. The cooking time will depend on the thickness of the fillets.

Remove from the oven, season with more pepper, squeeze the juice from one of the lemons over it, and scatter with the parsley.

Cut the remaining lemon into four wedges to serve with the fish.

Delicious with slices of buttered brown bread.

NOTE: *This recipe also works well with cod.*

2-quart Tagine

SERVES 4
Preparation time: 10 minutes
Cooking time: 1 hour 5 minutes

HADDOCK WITH FENNEL IN A CREAM SAUCE

Poached haddock with potatoes and fennel, cooked in fish stock with cream.

---

1 lb 2 oz new potatoes, scrubbed and cut into large dice

1 fennel bulb, sliced

Lovage or celery leaves from 2 stalks, chopped

2 bay leaves

⅔ cup fish stock

⅔ cup heavy cream

14 oz skinned and boned haddock, cut into large pieces

Salt and freshly ground black pepper

A few flat-leaf parsley sprigs, leaves coarsely chopped, to garnish

Place the potatoes, fennel, lovage or celery leaves, and bay leaves in the bottom of the tagine. Pour the fish stock and cream evenly over the vegetables and season with salt and pepper. Mix the ingredients together and cover with the lid. Cook over very low heat for 50 minutes, or until the potatoes are tender. Check occasionally to see if there is enough moisture in the tagine and, if needed, add some water as required.

Set the pieces of haddock on top of the potatoes, cover, and cook for a further 15 minutes over very low heat, or until the fish is cooked. Scatter the fish with the chopped parsley just before serving.

Rectangular Skillet Grill

GRILLED STUFFED MACKEREL WITH FRESH HERBS & CHEESE

**Fragrant fresh herbs and creamy soft cheese make
a light filling for fresh mackerel.**

SERVES 6
Preparation time: 15 minutes
Cooking time: 15 minutes

1 small egg, lightly beaten

1¼ cups cream cheese

A few mint sprigs, finely chopped

A few flat-leaf parsley sprigs, finely chopped, plus extra to garnish

A few dill sprigs, finely chopped

A few chervil sprigs, finely chopped

12 mackerel, gutted and cleaned

3 tablespoons olive oil

1 lemon, cut in half

Salt and freshly ground black pepper

Mix half of the beaten egg into the cream cheese. If the cheese is still firm, add more of the egg, but the mixture should not be too runny. Stir in the herbs and season with salt and pepper.

Stuff the mackerel, or fish of choice, with the cheese mixture and secure with kitchen string. Brush the mackerel with oil and season with pepper.

Heat the skillet grill over high heat, add the mackerel, and grill for 5 minutes on each side. (You may need to cook the fish in batches.) Grill the lemon at the same time, cut-side down.

Carefully cover the pan with foil and cook for a further 5 minutes over low heat until the filling is warmed through.

Place the mackerel on a serving plate and squeeze the juice of the lemons over it.

Serve with any leftover herb cheese sauce and a spinach and walnut salad, if liked.

NOTE: *This recipe also works well with herring, sardines or red mullet.*

BACON-WRAPPED TROUT WITH FENNEL & ANISEED

The combination of fennel, aniseed, and pastis add a distinctive flavor to the trout.

14½ x 12½-inch Rectangular
Stoneware Dish

SERVES 2 TO 4
Preparation time: 15 minutes
Cooking time: 40 minutes

½ stick butter

2 fennel bulbs, bulbs thinly sliced, fronds reserved

1 tablespoon pastis

1 tablespoon water

2 large trout, gutted and cleaned

4 slices of bacon

A few thyme sprigs

Salt and freshly ground black pepper

Chopped dill, to garnish (optional)

Preheat the oven to 315°F.

Add the butter to the stoneware dish and place in the oven until melted.

Arrange the fennel slices in the dish with the melted butter and season with salt and pepper.

Sprinkle the pastis and the measured water over the fennel and place in the oven for 15 minutes until softened.

Meanwhile, season the trout all over with pepper and wrap each one in two slices of bacon.

Increase the oven temperature to 325°F. Place the trout on top of the braised fennel, scatter with the thyme sprigs, and cook for a further 25 minutes until the fish is cooked.

Scatter the dish with the reserved fennel fronds or, if you don't have any fronds, finish with some chopped dill.

Cast Iron Rectangular Grill

ZUCCHINI & ANCHOVY BRUSCHETTA

Perfect as a summer appetizer.

SERVES 6

Preparation time: 5 minutes
Cooking time: 20 minutes

6 slices of ciabatta

Olive oil, for brushing

1½ tablespoons chile oil

Juice of 1 small lemon

1 zucchini, sliced lengthwise

6 anchovy fillets

1 teaspoon oregano leaves

Salt

Preheat the skillet grill over high heat.

Brush the ciabatta slices with the olive oil and grill on each side until golden brown.

Mix together the chile oil and three-quarters of the lemon juice, then brush the mixture over the zucchini slices and season with salt. Arrange the zucchini in the skillet grill and grill until blackened in places and tender. Remove and set aside.

Rub the anchovies with olive oil and grill for 5 minutes, turning once, or until cooked.

Top the ciabatta with the zucchini slices and anchovies. Squeeze the rest of the lemon juice over the bruschetta and sprinkle with the oregano leaves to serve.

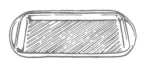

GRILLED SQUID WITH FENNEL & POMEGRANATE DRESSING

Packed with flavor, this warm squid salad features fresh lime, chile, herbs, and pomegranate.

Extra-Large Double Burner Grill

SERVES 6
Preparation time: 20 minutes
Cooking time: 15 minutes

1¾ lb whole squid, gutted and cleaned

2 fennel bulbs, bulbs sliced, fronds reserved

Olive oil, for brushing

Finely grated zest of 1 lime

1 red chile, seeded and finely chopped

1 handful of mint leaves, leaves chopped

1 handful of flat-leaf parsley, leaves chopped

2 red onions, sliced into rings

For the pomegranate dressing:

1 pomegranate, cut in half

½ cup olive oil

1 tablespoon honey

4 limes, cut in half

Salt and freshly ground black pepper

For the dressing, remove the pomegranate seeds by tapping the side of the fruit with a wooden spoon over a bowl. Collect any juices at the same time. Mix together the oil, 3 tablespoons of the pomegranate juice, and the honey until combined. Add 3 tablespoons of the pomegranate seeds.

Heat the double burner grill over medium heat.

Place the limes, cut-side down, on the grill pan and grill for 5 minutes. Remove and squeeze the juice from three of the limes into the dressing. Season with salt and pepper, taste, and add extra honey, if needed. Set the remaining lime aside.

Slice open the squid and cut in half. Using the tip of a sharp knife, lightly score a diamond pattern over each squid half, and season with a little salt and pepper.

Brush the fennel with some of the oil and season with salt and pepper. Place the fennel in the grill pan and chargrill for 5 minutes, turning once, until golden. Spoon the fennel onto a serving plate and scatter with the lime zest, chile, and herbs.

Brush the squid with oil and arrange it in the grill pan and chargrill for 1 to 2 minutes on each side, depending on its thickness (squid can become tough so do not overcook it). Remove from the heat, add the fennel, red onions, and fennel fronds to the squid. Drizzle with the dressing and serve immediately with the remaining lime.

3¾-quart Braiser

SERVES 4
Preparation time: 20 minutes
Cooking time: 35 minutes

COCONUT CLAM CURRY
Coconut lends a luxurious creaminess and tames the heat of the clam curry.

2 tablespoons peanut oil

6 cardamom pods, split

6 bay leaves

2 teaspoons mustard seeds

2 small cinnamon sticks

1 large onion, minced

4 garlic cloves, crushed

2 green chiles, seeded and finely diced

2 tablespoons ground cumin

2 tablespoons ground coriander

2 teaspoons ground turmeric

2¼ lb pumpkin or squash, peeled, seeded, and cut into 1-inch dice

½ cup water

1½ cups coconut milk

1 lb 5 oz clams, prepared, any clams with broken shells discarded

Salt

A few cilantro sprigs, to garnish

Heat the oil in the braiser over medium heat, add the cardamom, bay leaves, mustard seeds, and cinnamon sticks and fry for 1 to 2 minutes until the flavors are released.

Add the onion and garlic and continue to fry for 2 to 3 minutes. Stir in the chiles, cumin, coriander, and turmeric and cook for another 1 minute or until the onion is soft. Add the pumpkin or squash and cook for 5 minutes, stirring often.

Add the measured water and coconut milk. Bring to a boil, then turn the heat down and let simmer for 15 minutes, or until the sauce is reduced and the pumpkin or squash is tender. The flavor can be adjusted by adding extra coconut milk, ground cumin, and ground coriander to taste.

Stir the clams into the sauce, cover with the lid, and simmer until the clam shells open. Discard any unopened shells and season the sauce with salt.

Garnish with the cilantro sprigs and serve with boiled rice, if liked.

2-quart Tagine

SERVES 4
Preparation time: 20 minutes
Cooking time: 25 minutes

2 cooked brown female crabs, about 1¾ lb each

1 tablespoon olive oil

3 garlic cloves, chopped

1 cup dry white wine

¾-inch piece fresh ginger root, peeled and grated

2 bunches of cilantro, leaves chopped

½ teaspoon coriander seeds, ground

3 scallions, sliced diagonally, plus extra to garnish

1 red Thai chile, seeded and cut into fine strips

Juice of 2 limes

1 stick softened butter

1 tablespoon flour

Salt

CRAB WITH CILANTRO, CHILE & LIME

Delicious brown crab cooked in a fresh lime and cilantro butter sauce with a hint of chile.

To prepare the crabs, twist off the claws and legs, remove and discard the stomach sac and gray gills from the carapace (shell body), and reserve the crabmeat. Cut the crab body into large pieces.

Heat the oil in the bottom of the tagine over medium heat, add the garlic, and fry for 1 minute. Add the wine, bring to a boil, then turn the heat to low and cook until reduced.

Add the ginger, cilantro, ground coriander, scallions, chile, lime juice, crab legs, claws, and the crab shells to the tagine.

Combine the softened butter with the flour then stir it into in the tagine. Reduce the heat to very low, cover with the lid, and cook the crab for 20 minutes.

Season with salt and garnish with extra scallions. Serve with plenty of napkins!

4½- or 5½-quart Round Dutch Oven

CRAB-STUFFED BEEFSTEAK TOMATOES

Brimming with flavor, these ripe beefsteak tomatoes are filled with an herby crab mixture.

SERVES 4
Preparation time: 20 minutes
Cooking time: 35 minutes

5 beefsteak tomatoes

1 shallot, minced

2 garlic cloves, minced

2 to 3 thyme sprigs, leaves chopped

3 oregano sprigs, leaves chopped

2 to 3 rosemary sprigs, leaves picked and chopped

14 oz prepared crabmeat

1 slice of wholewheat bread, crusts removed, processed into crumbs

⅓ cup couscous

¾ cup vegetable stock

Salt and freshly ground black pepper

Preheat the oven to 400°F.

To prepare the tomatoes, cut off the top of each one and remove the pulp and seeds carefully with a spoon. Finely chop the pulp with the seeds and set aside.

To make the filling, mix together the shallot, garlic, herbs, crabmeat, bread crumbs, uncooked couscous, and the finely chopped tomato pulp. Season with salt and pepper.

Fill the tomatoes with the crab mixture, replace the tomato tops, and put them into the Dutch oven. Add the vegetable stock, cover with the lid, and bake in the oven for 30 to 35 minutes until the couscous is tender.

12½ x 9-inch Rectangular
Stoneware Dish

SERVES 4
Preparation time: 15 minutes
Cooking time: 20 minutes

LOBSTER WITH MOROCCAN SPICES

Treat yourselves to lobster in an aromatic spiced butter.

2 cooked lobsters, about 1½ lb each

1 stick butter

2 teaspoons ras el hanout

7 oz arugula

1 teaspoon olive oil

2 lemons, cut into wedges

Salt and freshly ground black pepper

Preheat the oven to 325°F.

Cut the lobsters in half and remove the stomach and the intestinal tract. Remove the rubber bands from the claws.

Add the butter to the dish and place in the oven until melted. Remove the dish from the oven and stir the ras el hanout into the melted butter.

Place the lobsters in the dish, spoon the spiced butter over them, and bake for 20 minutes until heated through.

Toss the arugula with the oil and season with salt and pepper.

Arrange the lobsters on a warm serving plate and drizzle the cooking juices over them. Top with the arugula salad and serve with the wedges of lemon.

A stick of crusty French bread goes well with the lobster.

2-quart Tagine

SERVES 4
Preparation time: 15 minutes
Cooking time: 20 minutes

SHRIMP WITH CHERMOULA
Jumbo shrimp infused with a spicy garlic and herb marinade and cooked in a tagine.

---

1 lb 2 oz raw unshelled jumbo shrimp, head and vein removed

For the chermoula:

2 garlic cloves, crushed

1 small bunch of flat-leaf parsley, leaves chopped

1 bunch of cilantro, leaves chopped

1 tablespoon mild paprika

1 teaspoon ground ginger

1 teaspoon ground cumin

Juice of 1 lemon

2 tablespoons olive oil

¼ teaspoon coarse sea salt

¼ to ½ teaspoon cayenne pepper or harissa paste, to taste

2 to 3 tablespoons water

For the chermoula, mix together all the ingredients in a medium-sized bowl, adding the cayenne or harissa paste to taste. Mix in enough of the measured water to make a thick sauce.

Stir in the prepared shrimp, ensuring they are coated in the chermoula. Then transfer everything to the bottom of the tagine and cover with the lid.

Place the tagine over low heat and cook the shrimp for 15 to 20 minutes, depending on their size, until cooked.

NOTE: *Harissa pastes can vary greatly in flavor and heat, so start with the smaller quantity first.*

7-inch Round Cast Iron Dish

SHRIMP SCAMPI WITH MUSHROOMS & ZUCCHINI

A simply delicious dish of baked shrimp scampi and vegetables—perfect for a light meal with crusty bread.

SERVES 4

Preparation time: 15 minutes
Cooking time: 20 minutes

---

16 to 24 raw shelled shrimp scampi, depending on size, head and vein removed, tail left on

2 tablespoons olive oil, divided

1 garlic clove, chopped

2 shallots, chopped

5½ oz shiitake mushrooms, sliced

5½ oz oyster mushrooms, sliced

5½ oz cremino mushrooms, sliced

5½ oz button mushrooms, sliced or left whole if small

1 zucchini, scooped into balls using a melon baller

Salt and freshly ground black pepper

1 tablespoon each of chopped chervil, dill, parsley, tarragon, and oregano, to garnish

Preheat the oven to 350°F.

Place the shrimp scampi in a bowl and season with salt and pepper. Add 1 tablespoon of the oil and stir to coat.

Heat the remaining oil in the cast iron dish over medium heat on the stove and add the garlic, shallots, mushrooms, and zucchini balls. Fry for 5 to 8 minutes, or until soft. Season with salt and pepper.

Scatter the vegetables with the shrimp scampi and place the dish in the oven for 10 minutes, or until the shrimp scampi are cooked.

Meanwhile, mix together all the herbs. Remove the shrimp scampi from the oven and scatter with the herbs before serving.

Square Skinny Griddle

MARINATED SHRIMP WITH FRESH HERB SAUCE

Packed with flavor, the shrimp are marinated in a chile, spice, and lime marinade and served with an herb yogurt sauce.

SERVES 6

Preparation time: 25 minutes, plus marinating
Cooking time: 10 minutes

2¾ lb raw shrimp, shelled or unshelled, depending on preference, vein removed

2 fresh lime leaves (optional)

2 limes, cut into wedges

For the spice marinade:

1 red chile, seeded and finely chopped

1 green chile, seeded and finely chopped

3 garlic cloves, chopped

½ teaspoon salt

1 handful of cilantro, leaves chopped

2 teaspoons ground cumin

2 teaspoons ground coriander

1 teaspoon paprika

3 tablespoons lime juice

¼ cup olive oil, divided, plus extra for brushing

For the fresh mint sauce:

A few mint sprigs, leaves finely chopped

A few cilantro sprigs, leaves finely chopped

1 red onion, minced

½ cup plain yogurt

1 teaspoon fish sauce

1 teaspoon lime juice

Freshly ground black pepper

For the spice marinade, grind the chiles, garlic, and salt in a mortar and pestle. Stir in the spices, lime juice, and enough of the olive oil to make a coarse paste.

Place the shrimp in a large nonmetallic dish, add the marinade, and stir to coat the shrimp. Cover and let marinate in the refrigerator for 3 hours, stirring occasionally.

Meanwhile, for the mint sauce, mix together all the ingredients in a bowl. Season with pepper, cover the bowl, and place in the fridge until ready to use.

Heat the griddle over medium heat and brush with oil. Add the lime leaves, if using. Using a slotted spoon, remove the shrimp from the marinade and place them in the pan. Griddle the shrimp for 5 to 8 minutes, turning once, until cooked.

Serve the shrimp with the mint sauce and wedges of lime. A baked potato and salad are good accompaniments, too.

VEGETABLE DISHES

RISOTTO WITH
A TRIO OF CHEESES

A tasty vegetarian risotto with a peppery arugula finish.

3¾-quart Braiser

SERVES 4
Preparation time: 15 minutes
Cooking time: 25 minutes

1 tablespoon olive oil

3 tablespoons butter, divided

2 shallots, minced

1 celery stalk, finely chopped

1¼ cups arborio risotto rice

⅓ cup dry sherry

4 cups hot vegetable stock

1 cup frozen peas

½ cup finely grated Parmesan cheese

1 oz blue cheese of choice

9 oz small mozzarella balls

1 handful of arugula

Freshly ground black pepper

Heat the oil and 2 tablespoons of the butter in the braiser over medium heat, add the shallots and celery, and fry for 2 to 3 minutes until softened. Stir in the rice. When all the grains are translucent, add the sherry and cook, stirring, until absorbed.

Add ½ cup of the hot stock and stir constantly, paying special attention to the bottom and the sides of the braiser, until absorbed by the rice. Now, add the stock a ladle at a time while continuing to stir. Wait for the stock to be absorbed before adding the next ladle of stock. Make sure the rice is kept at simmering point and, if needed, adjust the heat.

After 15 minutes, add the peas and continue stirring while adding the stock. After 20 minutes, test if the rice is "al dente," or almost cooked, and the risotto is a thick, soupy consistency. At this point, stir in the Parmesan, blue cheese, and the remaining butter and remove the pan from the heat.

Season with pepper and just before serving, stir in the mozzarella balls, and top with the arugula.

8-inch Square Stoneware Dish

SERVES 4
Preparation time: 15 minutes
Cooking time: 40 minutes

RICE WITH MEDITERRANEAN VEGETABLES

Delicious as a side dish to a meat, fish, or vegetarian meal.

½ zucchini, cut into ¼-inch cubes

½ eggplant, cut into ¼-inch cubes

½ fennel bulb, cut into ¼-inch cubes

½ red bell pepper, seeded and cut into ¼-inch cubes

½ green bell pepper, seeded and cut into ¼-inch cubes

1 red onion, minced

2 plum tomatoes, diced

2 garlic cloves, minced

2 tablespoons olive oil

1 tablespoon herbes de Provence

¾ cup long-grain rice

4 cups chicken stock

Salt and freshly ground black pepper

Basil leaves, to garnish

Preheat the oven to 315°F.

Mix all the vegetables with the oil, herbes de Provence, and rice, season with salt and pepper, and spoon the mixture into the stoneware dish. Roast for 10 minutes, or until the vegetables are starting to soften.

Remove the dish from the oven, then add the stock and stir well.

Return the dish to the oven, cover with foil, and cook for a further 30 minutes, stirring frequently, until the rice is tender. Garnish with basil before serving.

SPRING VEGETABLE CASSEROLE

Fava beans and asparagus mean spring is in the air!

4½-quart Round Dutch Oven

SERVES 4
Preparation time: 10 minutes
Cooking time: 15 minutes

1 tablespoon olive oil

2 garlic cloves, crushed

1½-inch piece fresh ginger root, peeled and grated

½ cup sherry

½ cup dry bulgur wheat

14 asparagus spears, woody ends discarded

1 lb 2 oz fava beans, shelled

5 scallions, finely chopped

1⅓ cup frozen peas

2 bay leaves

2½ cups vegetable or chicken stock

Salt and freshly ground black pepper

1 small handful of parsley and mint, leaves chopped, to garnish

Heat the oil in the Dutch oven over medium heat, add the garlic and ginger, and fry for 1 minute. Pour in the sherry and cook until reduced.

Add the bulgur wheat, asparagus, fava beans, scallions, peas, and bay leaves and fry for 4 minutes, stirring. Add the stock, stir, and cover with the lid. Simmer for 10 to 12 minutes until the vegetables are tender and the bulgur is cooked.

Season with salt and pepper and garnish with the parsley and mint just before serving.

CHICKPEA & SPINACH CASSEROLE

A quick, lightly spiced vegetarian casserole, full of healthy ingredients.

2-quart Round Dutch Oven

SERVES 4
Preparation time: 10 minutes
Cooking time: 15 minutes

1 tablespoon vegetable oil

1 red onion, chopped

2 garlic cloves, crushed

1 small green chile, seeded and chopped

2 teaspoons ground ginger

¼ to ½ teaspoon sea salt

2 x 14 oz cans chickpeas, drained

1 teaspoon ground cumin

½ teaspoon ground turmeric

⅓ cup water

9 oz cherry tomatoes, cut in half

5½ oz baby spinach

1 tablespoon lemon juice

Salt and freshly ground black pepper

Heat the oil in the Dutch oven over medium heat, add the onion, garlic, chile, ginger, and sea salt and fry for 5 minutes until the onion is soft.

Stir in the chickpeas, cumin, and turmeric and season with pepper. Add the measured water and stir until it has been absorbed.

Add the cherry tomatoes and cook for a further 3 minutes. Remove from the heat and add the spinach and lemon juice, stirring until the leaves have wilted. Taste and season with extra salt and pepper, if needed.

2- or 4½-quart Round Dutch Oven

SPICED ROASTED BELL PEPPER SOUP

The roasted bellpeppers give this soup a smoky sweetness and vibrant color.

SERVES 4

Preparation time: 15 minutes
Cooking time: 40 minutes

6 large ripe tomatoes

1 tablespoon olive oil

1 red onion, minced

1 red chile, seeded and finely chopped

2½ cups drained roasted red bell peppers from a jar, rinsed and chopped

4 thyme sprigs, divided

1 bay leaf

1 tablespoon curry powder

2½ cups vegetable stock

A splash of heavy cream (optional)

Salt and freshly ground black pepper

To skin the tomatoes, put them in a bowl and add boiling water to cover. Let stand for 1 to 2 minutes, then drain, cut a cross at the stem end of each tomato, and peel off the skin. Remove and discard the seeds, coarsely chop the tomato pulp, then set aside.

Heat the oil in the Dutch oven over medium heat, add the onion and chile, and fry for 2 to 3 minutes until softened. Add the roasted bell peppers and chopped tomatoes, three of the thyme sprigs, the bay leaf, and curry powder and cook for a further 5 minutes.

Pour in the stock, cover with the lid, and cook for 30 minutes over low heat.

Remove the bay leaf and thyme sprigs. Transfer the soup to a blender or food processor and blend until smooth.

Return the soup to the Dutch oven, heat through, and season with salt and pepper. Serve topped with cream, if liked, and the remaining sprig of thyme.

NOTE: *Instead of using roasted bell peppers from a jar, you could roast your own. For this soup, brush 6 bell peppers with olive oil (and reduce the quantity of tomatoes to three). Place on a hot skillet grill and chargrill, turning occasionally, until the skins begin to blister and blacken. Place the roasted bell peppers in a bowl, cover with plastic wrap, and let cool. Peel off the skins, retaining any juices, then remove the seeds and cut the bell peppers into slices. You could also roast the bell peppers in the oven or under a broiler.*

4 x Mini Round Cocottes

EGGS EN COCOTTE WITH ASPARAGUS

A simply delicious breakfast, light meal, or snack.

SERVES 4
Preparation time: 5 minutes
Cooking time: 15 minutes

---

2 teaspoons melted butter

8 small asparagus spears,
woody ends discarded, cut in half

4 large eggs

Salt and freshly ground black pepper

Crusty bread and watercress sprigs,
to serve

Preheat the oven to 400°CF

Grease the individual cocottes with the melted butter and add some salt and pepper.

Place the asparagus pieces into the bottom of the cocottes and break an egg into each one. Season again with salt and pepper.

Lay a sheet of parchment paper in a deep stoneware dish or roasting pan that is large enough to hold the cocottes. Place the cocottes into the dish or pan and add enough hot water to come two-thirds of the way up the sides. Place the dish in the oven and cook for 15 minutes, or until the eggs are cooked to your liking.

Serve with crusty bread and watercress on the side.

2-quart Tagine

SERVES 4
Preparation time: 15 minutes
Cooking time: 55 minutes

SWEET BELL PEPPERS WITH EGGS

A tasty dish, perfect for a weekend brunch.

4 tomatoes

2 tablespoons olive oil

1 large red onion, minced

2 garlic cloves, chopped

6 mixed bell peppers (red, yellow, and orange), seeded, stalks removed, and sliced

1 small red or green chile, seeded and finely chopped

1 teaspoon fennel seeds

½ cup water

4 eggs

Salt and freshly ground black pepper

To skin the tomatoes, put them in a bowl and add boiling water to cover. Let stand for 1 to 2 minutes, then drain, cut a cross at the stem end of each tomato, and peel off the skin. Remove the seeds, dice the tomatoes, and set to one side.

Heat the oil in the bottom of the tagine over medium heat, add the onion and garlic, and fry for 5 minutes until the onion is soft.

Add the sliced bell peppers, chile, and fennel seeds. Season with salt and pepper. Stir in the diced tomatoes and the measured water. Reduce the heat to low, cover with the lid, and cook for 45 minutes, stirring occasionally.

Five minutes before the end of the cooking time, make 4 spaces in the vegetables with the back of a spoon. Break in the eggs, replace the lid, and continue to cook until the eggs are set. Serve the tagine immediately.

NOTE: *You could try using a mixture of baby bell peppers and quail eggs.*

2-quart Tagine

SERVES 4
Preparation time: 10 minutes
Cooking time: 1½ hours

SLOW-COOKED TOMATOES WITH HONEY & CINNAMON

Serve these sweet-spiced tomatoes warm or cold with cold cuts or cheeses.

2¼ lb tomatoes, a mixture of different varieties, colors, and sizes

¼ cup olive oil, divided

2 cinnamon sticks, cut in half lengthwise

3 bay leaves

½ teaspoon ground turmeric

1 tablespoon coarsely chopped thyme

2 tablespoons honey

Salt and freshly ground black pepper

Prepare the tomatoes by cutting some of them in half and removing the seeds of the larger ones with a teaspoon.

Pour 2 tablespoons of the oil into the bottom of the tagine and add the tomatoes. Place the cinnamon sticks and the bay leaves between the tomatoes.

In a small bowl, mix together the turmeric, thyme, honey, and the remaining 2 tablespoons of oil. Spoon the mixture over the tomatoes, season with salt and pepper, and cover with the lid.

Place the tagine over very low heat and cook the tomatoes for 1½ hours, or until tender. Check occasionally that the tomatoes are not sticking to the bottom and, if needed, add a little water. Serve warm or cold in the tagine.

Reversible Grill/Griddle

SERVES 6
Preparation time: 10 minutes
Cooking time: 25 minutes

OREGANO & RICOTTA-STUFFED TOMATOES

Serve as a side dish with barbecued food, or as a main with new potatoes.

6 large firm tomatoes, cut in half

1 tablespoon olive oil

¾ cup ricotta cheese

2¼ oz spinach, finely chopped

1 teaspoon dried oregano

Freshly grated nutmeg, to taste

2 tablespoons pine nuts

2 slices of bread, crusts removed and processed into crumbs

½ cup finely grated Parmesan cheese

Salt and freshly ground black pepper

Brush the cut half of each tomato with the oil and season with salt and pepper.

Mix together the ricotta, spinach, oregano, and nutmeg in a bowl and season with salt and pepper.

Heat the pan over medium heat, smooth-side up, and toast the pine nuts until starting to color. Remove the nuts from the pan and set aside.

Griddle the bread crumbs in the same pan until toasted then remove, set aside, and wipe the pan clean.

Return the pan to the heat and griddle the halved tomatoes, cut-side down, until slightly blackened. Turn them over and top with a good spoonful of the ricotta mixture. Sprinkle with the Parmesan.

Cover with foil, making sure it does not touch the tomatoes. Turn the heat to low and cook the tomatoes for 8 to 10 minutes until warmed through but still holding their shape.

Scatter the tomatoes with the bread crumbs and pine nuts before serving.

You could serve the tomatoes with a spinach salad.

EGGPLANTS STUFFED WITH RICE, HERBS & PINE NUTS

Healthy, light, and nutritious—perfect as an appetizer or light meal.

2-quart Tagine

SERVES 4
Preparation time: 15 minutes, plus salting
Cooking time: 55 minutes

2 small eggplants,
cut in half lengthwise

Coarse sea salt, for salting

3 tablespoons olive oil, divided

½ onion, minced

1 garlic clove, chopped

½ bunch of chives, leaves chopped

½ bunch of dill, leaves chopped

½ bunch of flat-leaf parsley,
leaves chopped

¼ cup toasted pine nuts

1 teaspoon dried mint

½ cup cooked white rice

½ teaspoon mild paprika

¾ cup water, plus extra as required

Juice of 1 small lemon

Salt and freshly ground black pepper

Dill sprigs, to garnish

To prepare the eggplants, carefully scoop out the pulp with a spoon and set the halves to one side. Coarsely chop the pulp and place it in a sieve. Sprinkle with coarse sea salt and place the sieve over a sink for 30 minutes.

Rinse the eggplant pulp thoroughly under cold running water, then drain and pat dry with paper towels.

Heat 2 tablespoons of the oil in the bottom of the tagine over medium-low heat and fry the onion and garlic until soft. Add the eggplant pulp and fry for 8 to 10 minutes until starting to turn golden.

Spoon the cooked eggplant mixture into a bowl and stir in the herbs, pine nuts, dried mint, cooked rice, and paprika. Season with salt and pepper.

Spoon the herb mixture into the eggplant halves. Place them in the bottom of the tagine with the filling upward and carefully pour in the measured water, the remaining oil, and the lemon juice.

Cover with the lid and set the tagine over low heat for 40 minutes until the stuffed eggplants are cooked through. Check occasionally that the eggplants are not sticking to the bottom and, if needed, add a little extra water.

Garnish with sprigs of dill and serve with pitta bread, if you like.

Cast Iron Rectangular Grill

EGGPLANT, PESTO & MOZZARELLA STACKS

Slices of pesto-coated eggplant are filled with mozzarella and fresh basil then cooked in a broiler pan until golden—delicious!

SERVES 6
Preparation time: 15 minutes, plus salting
Cooking time: 10 minutes

---

4 eggplants, cut into 24 slices, each ½ inch in thickness, ends discarded

9 oz buffalo mozzarella, drained and cut into 12 slices

12 large basil leaves, plus extra to garnish

12 cherry tomatoes, cut in half

For the pesto:

½ cup finely grated Parmesan cheese

2 handfuls of basil

1 garlic clove

⅔ cup olive oil

½ cup pine nuts

Juice of 1 lemon

Salt and freshly ground black pepper

Sprinkle the eggplant slices with salt and let stand for 30 minutes, then rinse under cold running water and pat dry.

Meanwhile, make the pesto: put all the ingredients, except the lemon juice, in a blender and blend until finely chopped. Add the lemon juice and season with salt and pepper.

Brush one side of each eggplant slice with pesto.

Place 12 of the eggplant slices, pesto-side down, on a sheet of parchment paper or a cookie sheet and top each one with a slice of mozzarella, a basil leaf, and two halves of cherry tomato. Season with pepper. Place a second slice of eggplant on top, pesto-side up, to make a "sandwich" and press firmly together.

Heat the skillet grill over high heat, add the eggplant stacks, and chargrill for 5 minutes on each side until tender and golden. Garnish with extra basil and serve immediately.

3¾-quart Braiser

SERVES 4
Preparation time: 15 minutes
Cooking time: 20 minutes

EGGPLANT SALSA

An eggplant salsa with plenty of zing—serve as a side dish or as a meal with couscous or rice.

2 tablespoons olive oil,
plus extra if required

3 large eggplants, cut into slices
1½ to 2 inches long

4 oregano sprigs

2 red onions, cut into wedges

2 garlic cloves, crushed

2 tablespoons capers in vinegar,
drained

¼ cup white wine vinegar

1 tablespoon balsamic vinegar

2 tablespoons extra-virgin olive oil

2 tablespoons shelled unsalted
pistachios, chopped

1¾ oz Parmesan cheese,
sliced into shavings

Salt and freshly ground black pepper

Heat the oil in the braiser over medium heat, add the eggplant slices and oregano, and fry, stirring, for 3 to 4 minutes until browned on all sides.

Add the onions and garlic and fry for a further 3 to 4 minutes, adding a little extra oil if the braiser is too dry.

Stir in the capers and wine vinegar, cover with the lid, and cook over low heat for 10 minutes, or until the vegetables are tender. Season with salt and pepper.

Drizzle the balsamic vinegar and extra-virgin olive oil evenly all over the salsa and scatter with the pistachios and Parmesan shavings.

Couscous or rice make good accompaniments.

1-or 2-quart Round Dutch Oven

SERVES 4
Preparation time: 15 minutes, plus cooling
Cooking time: 50 minutes

PEA SOUFFLÉ

A warm and comforting soufflé made in a Dutch oven.

1 lb 2 oz fresh peas, shelled

2 tablespoons butter, plus extra for greasing

3 tablespoons all-purpose flour

1 cup milk

Freshly grated nutmeg, to taste

2 large eggs, separated

½ cup finely grated Parmesan cheese

2 tablespoons chopped basil leaves

½ cup bread crumbs

⅓ cup pine nuts

Salt and freshly ground black pepper

Preheat the oven to 350°F.

Cook the peas in the Dutch oven in lightly salted water until tender. Drain and rinse them immediately under cold running water to keep their bright green color. Purée the cooked peas in a blender until smooth and season with salt and pepper. Set to one side.

To make a béchamel sauce, melt the butter in the Dutch oven over low heat. Add the flour and cook for 1 minute, stirring. Add the milk, a little at a time, stirring continuously, until you have a smooth, creamy sauce. Grate in the nutmeg, to taste, and season with salt and pepper. Pour the sauce into a pitcher and let cool.

Combine the egg yolks with the pea purée, Parmesan, and basil and stir the mixture into the cooled béchamel sauce until combined. Beat the egg whites in a clean bowl until they form stiff peaks then fold them into the egg yolk and pea mixture.

Wash and dry the Dutch oven then grease the inside with the extra butter and dust with the bread crumbs.

Pour the soufflé mixture into the Dutch oven. Scatter with the pine nuts and cook for 40 minutes, or until puffed up and golden. To check if it is ready, pierce with a skewer. If it comes out dry, the soufflé is cooked.

Serve immediately.

5-quart Oval Dutch Oven

ITALIAN BRAISED VEGETABLES

Braised vegetables that capture the authentic flavors of the Mediterranean.

SERVES 6
Preparation time: 20 minutes
Cooking time: 40 minutes

6 baby artichokes

Juice of 1 lemon

3 tablespoons olive oil

2 lemons, cut into wedges

2 garlic cloves, minced

3 to 4 lemon thyme sprigs

2 bay leaves

1 fennel bulb, cut into 8 pieces, green fronds reserved and chopped

¾ lb baby new potatoes, scrubbed and cut in half

3 tablespoons Pernod Ricard

½ cup vegetable stock

A pinch of saffron threads

Salt and freshly ground black pepper

Cut the stems from the artichokes, remove the tough outer leaves, trim the tips, then cut them in half. Add the lemon juice to some water in a bowl and plunge the artichokes into the liquid to prevent them from discoloring. Set aside.

Heat the oil in the Dutch oven over medium heat, add the lemon wedges, garlic, lemon thyme, and bay leaves and cook, stirring for 2 to 3 minutes. Stir in the fennel and potatoes.

Drain the artichokes, add them to the Dutch oven, and cook for a few more minutes. Pour in the Pernod Ricard and cook until reduced, then add the stock and saffron and bring the contents to a boil.

Reduce the heat, cover with the lid, and simmer for 30 to 35 minutes until the potatoes are tender, adding extra stock, if necessary. Season to taste with salt and pepper, and serve garnished with the reserved fennel fronds.

PROVENÇAL ROASTED VEGETABLES

Typical of Provence, this medley of roasted vegetables can be served warm or cold as a salad.

9½ x 7½-inch Rectangular
Stoneware Dish

SERVES 4
Preparation time: 20 minutes
Cooking time: 45 minutes

2 garlic cloves, peeled and cut in half

3 tablespoons olive oil

1 tablespoon herbes de Provence

1 red chile, seeded and thinly sliced

2 red onions, cut into wedges

2 red bell peppers, seeded
and cut into wedges

2 green bell peppers, seeded
and cut into wedges

1 eggplant, cut into quarters,
and each quarter into wedges

1 zucchini, thickly sliced

½ fennel bulb, cut into wedges

2 plum tomatoes, cut in half

2 large mushrooms, cut into quarters

1 teaspoon coarse sea salt

Preheat the oven to 315°F.

Mix the garlic with the oil, herbs, and chile.

Put the onions, red and green bell peppers, eggplant, zucchini, fennel, tomatoes, and mushrooms in the stoneware dish, drizzle with the flavored oil, and stir gently to coat. Season with the coarse sea salt.

Roast in the oven for 45 minutes, turning occasionally, until the vegetables are cooked. Serve warm or cold as a salad.

ASPARAGUS WITH SAFFRON CREAM

Asparagus in a saffron-scented creamy sauce.

2-quart Tagine

SERVES 4
Preparation time: 10 minutes
Cooking time: 25 minutes

---

1 tablespoon olive oil

24 white or green asparagus spears, woody ends discarded, stems peeled

A generous pinch of saffron threads

½ cup vegetable stock

½ cup light cream

Salt and freshly ground black pepper

Heat the oil in the bottom of the tagine over medium heat, add the asparagus, and sauté on all sides until lightly colored. Add the saffron and the vegetable stock and season with salt and pepper.

Place the lid on the tagine, reduce the heat to low, and cook the asparagus for 15 to 20 minutes, depending on their size, until tender.

Divide the asparagus among 4 preheated serving plates. Add the cream to the stock in the tagine and heat gently until warm but not hot.

Adjust the seasoning to taste, then pour the sauce over the asparagus. Serve immediately.

2-quart Tagine

SERVES 4
Preparation time: 15 minutes
Cooking time: 50 minutes

MOROCCAN-SPICED HEIRLOOM CARROTS

The Moroccan spice mixture, ras el hanout, complements the sweet taste of the striking heirloom carrots.

3 tablespoons olive oil

1½ lb heirloom carrots (purple, yellow, and white), cut in half lengthwise, then cut into 4 diagonal pieces

2 garlic cloves, peeled and left whole

1 teaspoon ras el hanout

A pinch of chili powder

3 tablespoons currants

2 bay leaves

⅔ cup water

Juice of 1 small lemon

½ bunch of flat-leaf parsley, leaves chopped

½ bunch of cilantro, leaves chopped

3 tablespoons toasted pine nuts

Salt

Heat 2 tablespoons of the oil in the bottom of the tagine over low heat. Add the carrots, garlic, ras el hanout, chili powder, currants, bay leaves, and the measured water. Mix everything together, cover with the lid, and cook the carrots for 50 minutes, or until they are tender.

Remove the garlic from the tagine and crush with the lemon juice and the remaining oil in a mortar and pestle until smooth.

Add the garlic and lemon paste to the cooked carrots and stir in the parsley, cilantro, and toasted pine nuts.

Season to taste with salt and serve.

2-quart Tagine

SERVES 4
Preparation time: 15 minutes, plus soaking
Cooking time: 40 minutes

⅔ cup warm water

2 teaspoons orange-flower water

3 tablespoons raisins

1 tablespoon olive oil

1 small onion, minced

1 teaspoon ras el hanout

½ teaspoon ground cumin

⅔ cup vegetable stock

1¾ lb butternut squash, cut in half, seeded, and cut into thick slices

1 cinnamon stick

3 tablespoons blanched almonds, coarsely chopped

Salt and freshly ground black pepper

SPICED SQUASH WITH RAISINS
A colorful and fragrant dish with a hint of Moroccan spice—perfect as a side dish for roasted meats and fish.

Pour the warm water into a bowl, stir in the orange-flower water and the raisins, and let stand for 30 minutes.

Heat the oil in the bottom of the tagine over medium heat, add the onion, and fry until lightly caramelized.

Mix together the ras el hanout, cumin, and vegetable stock. Season with salt and pepper and stir the mixture into the caramelized onion.

Place the squash slices in the tagine and add the cinnamon stick and the soaked, drained raisins. Cover with the lid, reduce the heat to low, and cook the squash for 40 minutes, or until tender.

Scatter the squash with the almonds just before serving.

2-quart Tagine

SERVES 4
Preparation time: 10 minutes
Cooking time: 1 hour

BRAISED BELGIAN ENDIVES WITH HONEY & ORANGE
Tender endives finished with a butter, honey, and orange glaze.

8 large Belgian endives, cut into 2 or 3, depending on size, core discarded

1 cup vegetable stock

2 tablespoons honey

3 tablespoons butter

½ teaspoon pared orange zest

1 tablespoon olive oil

Salt and freshly ground black pepper

Arrange the Belgian endives in the bottom of the tagine and pour the vegetable stock evenly over them. Season with salt and pepper. Cover with the lid and cook for 50 minutes over low heat.

Remove the lid and add the honey, butter, orange zest, and oil. Increase the heat to medium and cook the endives, without the lid, for a further 10 minutes, turning them occasionally until caramelized on all sides. Serve in the tagine.

2-quart Tagine

SERVES 4
Preparation time: 10 minutes
Cooking time: 1 hour

CAULIFLOWER WITH SLICED GARLIC

Simple braised whole cauliflower with fried slices of garlic.

1¼ cups water, plus extra as required

1 teaspoon ground turmeric

1 tablespoon olive oil,
plus extra for frying

1 cauliflower, outer leaves and
woody stem removed, blanched
for 10 minutes

7 garlic cloves, thinly sliced

Salt and freshly ground
black pepper

Heat enough oil to generously cover the bottom of a small skillet. Add the sliced garlic to the hot oil and fry quickly until golden brown, while shaking the pan. Remove the slices with a slotted spoon, drain on paper towels, season with salt and pepper and set aside. Wipe the base of the tagine clean.

Mix together the measured water, ground turmeric, and 1 tablespoon of the oil in a bowl and season to taste with salt and pepper. Place the cauliflower in the bottom of the tagine, add the turmeric mixture, and cover with the lid.

Place the tagine over very low heat and cook the cauliflower for approximately 1 hour, or until tender. Check occasionally that the cauliflower is not dry and, if needed, add a little extra water.

Serve the cauliflower, scattered with the fried garlic slices, in the tagine.

DESSERTS

POACHED PEARS IN WINE, HONEY & GINGER

Sweet pears poached in wine with honey, ginger, and a hint of spice.

2-quart Tagine

SERVES 6
Preparation time: 10 minutes
Cooking time: 1 hour 20 minutes

6 firm ripe pears, such as Bartlett or Anjou, peeled and stalks left on

2 tablespoons lemon juice

1¼ cups sweet white wine

½-inch piece fresh ginger root, peeled and thinly sliced

½ teaspoon ground black peppercorns

2 tablespoons soft brown sugar

2 tablespoons mild-tasting honey

2 tablespoons butter

To prepare the pears, carefully remove the core from the base of each one and brush all over with the lemon juice to stop the fruit from discoloring.

Place the cored pears upright in the bottom of the tagine and pour the wine over them. Place on the stove over medium heat and bring the wine to a boil.

Add the ginger, peppercorns, sugar, honey, and butter. Cover with the lid, reduce the heat to low, and poach the pears for 1 hour to 1 hour 20 minutes, depending on their size and degree of ripeness. Occasionally baste the pears with the cooking juices while cooking.

Serve the pears in the tagine or in warmed bowls.

Square Skinny Griddle

CARAMELIZED ORCHARD FRUIT WITH CALVADOS SAUCE

The Normandy apple brandy, Calvados, adds the finishing touch to this dessert.

SERVES 6
Preparation time: 10 minutes
Cooking time: 25 minutes

1 vanilla bean, sliced lengthwise and seeds scraped out

3 tablespoons superfine sugar

1 teaspoon ground cinnamon

3 tablespoons melted butter

3 apples, cored and cut into quarters

3 pears, cored and cut into quarters

3 tablespoons Calvados

2 tablespoons roasted hazelnuts

Mix the vanilla seeds, sugar, and cinnamon with the melted butter.

Brush the apples and pears with the spiced butter.

Heat the griddle over medium heat, add the apples and pears, and cook, turning occasionally, until caramelized. Remove the pan from the heat, pour in the Calvados, then flambé the fruit. Let cool slightly.

Cover the pan with a lid or foil and cook for a further 8 to 10 minutes over low heat. Serve the fruit with any pan juices drizzled over it, and scattered with roasted hazelnuts.

The caramelized fruit is also delicious served on a pancake with a scoop of ice cream.

2-quart Tagine

SERVES 4
Preparation time: 10 minutes
Cooking time: 1½ hours

FIVE-SPICE & VANILLA POACHED APPLES

Sweet spice and vanilla-infused apples—perfect with ice cream or thick plain yogurt.

2 tablespoons butter, diced

4 apples, cored and sliced

1 vanilla bean, split lengthwise and seeds scraped out

⅓ cup superfine sugar

⅓ teaspoon Chinese five-spice powder

⅔ cup water, plus extra as required

Place the butter in the bottom of the tagine and arrange the apples on top.

Mix the vanilla seeds with the sugar and five-spice powder, then sprinkle the mixture evenly over the apples. Add the measured water to the apples and cover with the lid.

Place the tagine over very low heat and poach the apples for 1½ hours. Check occasionally that there is enough moisture in the tagine and, if needed, add extra water as required.

Serve the apples warm or at room temperature with yogurt or ice cream.

9¾-inch Round Tarte Tatin Pan,
or Stoneware Round Pie Dish

SERVES 4
Preparation time: 15 minutes
Cooking time: 30 minutes

TARTE TATIN
Everyone's favorite classic French apple dessert!

½ stick butter (unsalted, if available)

4 apples, peeled, cut in half, cored, and cut into ½-inch thick slices

½ cup superfine sugar

1 sheet of ready-made puff pastry

Preheat the oven to 425°F.

Add the butter to the tatin pan and place in the oven until the butter has melted. Swirl the melted butter around in the pan to ensure the bottom is completely covered.

Arrange the apple slices in the pan. Sprinkle with the sugar, return the pan to the oven, and bake until the apples are soft and caramelized.

Meanwhile, unroll the pastry and cut it into a 10-inch disk. Prick the pastry all over with a fork and carefully place the pastry on top of the apples. Tuck the pastry over the apples and down the inside of the pan. Return it to the oven for another 15 minutes, or until the pastry is cooked and golden.

Let cool slightly. Then, wearing oven mitts, carefully but quickly invert the pan onto a large plate, so the caramelized apples are on top. Serve warm with cream or ice cream.

BLOOD ORANGES
WITH CAMPARI & HONEY

A simple dessert of blood oranges with a hint of spice.

2-quart Tagine

SERVES 4
Preparation time: 15 minutes
Cooking time: 1½ hours

14 fl oz Campari

1 cup water

3 tablespoons orange blossom honey

1 bay leaf

2 black peppercorns

4 blood oranges, peeled

Pour the Campari and the measured water into the bottom of the tagine. Add the honey, bay leaf, and peppercorns and bring the contents to a boil over medium heat.

Add the oranges to the tagine, reduce the heat to low, cover with the lid, and poach the oranges for 1½ hours, or until tender.

Serve the oranges in dessert bowls, drizzled with some of the poaching juices.

ALMOND PUDDING WITH PINK GRAPEFRUIT

Caramel-topped almond pudding with a citrus base.

2-quart Tagine

SERVES 4
Preparation time: 15 minutes
Cooking time: 35 minutes

Butter, for greasing

3 pink grapefruit,
peeled and segmented

2 eggs

½ cup superfine sugar,
plus extra for dusting

1½ cups ground almonds

1 cup heavy whipping cream

1 tablespoon orange-flower water

½ vanilla bean, split lengthwise
and seeds scraped out

Freshly ground black pepper

Preheat the oven to 350°F.

Grease the bottom inside of the tagine with butter and add the grapefruit segments, arranging them into a fan shape.

In a mixing bowl, beat the eggs with the sugar until light and fluffy. Fold in the ground almonds, heavy whipping cream, orange-flower water, and vanilla seeds, then add a grinding of pepper on top.

Pour the mixture evenly over the grapefruit segments in the tagine. Cover with the lid and bake for 30 minutes.

Toward the end of the cooking time, preheat the broiler to high. Remove the lid from the tagine and sprinkle the pudding with a thin layer of sugar. Place the (uncovered) tagine under the broiler to caramelize the sugar; keep an eye on it to stop it from burning.

Serve the dessert warm in the tagine or let cool before serving.

9 x 7-inch Rectangular Stoneware Dish

SERVES 4
Preparation time: 10 minutes
Cooking time: 15 minutes

CARAMELIZED PINEAPPLE WITH KIRSCH

The cherry liqueur adds a kick to the caramelized sauce for the pineapple.

½ stick butter (unsalted, if available)

¼ cup superfine sugar

3 tablespoons kirsch

1 pineapple, skin removed, cored, and cut into chunks

⅔ cup mixed dried berries and raisins

1 cup slivered almonds

Mint sprigs, to decorate

Preheat the oven to 350°F.

Add the butter to the stoneware dish and place in the oven. When the butter has melted remove the dish from the oven and stir in the sugar. Return to the oven for 5 minutes until caramelized.

Add the kirsch to the dish and stir in the pineapple, mixed berries and raisins, and the almonds.

Preheat the broiler to medium-high, then broil the pineapple for 5 minutes until starting to color.

Remove the dish from the oven and serve the pineapple with a scoop of coconut ice cream, decorated with mint sprigs.

Round Skillet Grill

GRILLED PEACHES WITH AMARETTO & AMARETTI CRISP

Two Italian indulgences in one irresistible dessert!

SERVES 6
Preparation time: 10 minutes, plus marinating
Cooking time: 10 minutes

---

6 fresh peaches,
or the equivalent canned

½ cup Amaretto

½ cup mascarpone

⅔ cup cream cheese

2 tablespoons confectioners' sugar

Butter, for greasing

6 amaretti cookies, crumbled

Peel the fresh peaches, then cut them in half and remove the stones. If you are using canned peaches, drain them first and pat dry. Put the peaches in a dish, pour the Amaretto over them, and let them marinate for 5 to 10 minutes.

Mix together the mascarpone, cream cheese, and confectioners' sugar in a bowl. Cover and chill in the refrigerator until ready to serve.

Heat the skillet grill and grease with butter. Remove the peaches from the Amaretto and discard the marinade.

Grill the fresh peaches for 7 to 10 minutes (4 to 5 minutes for canned peaches), turning once. Spoon the mascarpone mixture on top of the peaches and serve scattered with the crushed amaretti cookies.

2-quart Tagine

RED PLUMS WITH PINK PEPPERCORNS

A delicious summer treat—ripe plums served with a scoop or two of rich vanilla ice cream.

SERVES 4
Preparation time: 10 minutes
Cooking time: 40 minutes

10 red plums, cut in half and pitted

1 tablespoon olive oil

½ cup superfine sugar

1 teaspoon pink peppercorns, crushed

1 vanilla bean, split lengthwise and seeds scraped out

½ cup water

Place the plums in the bottom of the tagine. Stir in the oil, sugar, pink peppercorns, vanilla seeds, and the measured water.

Cover with the lid and poach the plums over very low heat for 30 to 40 minutes until soft.

Remove the plums with a slotted spoon and set aside. Increase the heat to medium and cook the juices in the tagine until reduced and slightly thickened.

Return the plums to the tagine and serve with ice cream.

10-inch Round Skillet Grill

GRILLED MELON WITH THYME, HONEY & LIME

A light, fresh, and fruity dessert—perfect for hot days.

SERVES 6
Preparation time: 10 minutes, plus marinating
Cooking time: 2 minutes

2 tablespoons honey

A few lemon thyme sprigs

Juice of 1 lime

2 tablespoons melted butter

A large pinch of freshly ground
Szechuan pepper

1 muskmelon, cut in half, seeded,
and each half cut into 6 slices

For the marinade, mix together the honey, lemon thyme, lime juice, and melted butter in a large shallow dish until combined. Season with Szechuan pepper.

Add the melon to the dish, spoon the marinade evenly over it, cover, and let marinate in the refrigerator for 1 hour.

Heat the skillet grill over medium heat. Brush the melon slices with the excess marinade and grill for 1 to 2 minutes, turning once, until golden in places.

Serve with thick yogurt or sour cream.

10-inch Oval Cast Iron Dish

SERVES 4
Preparation time: 15 minutes
Cooking time: 15 minutes

STICKY FRUIT KEBABS

A delicious and colorful way to serve fruit.

½ apple, peeled, cored, and cut into equal-sized pieces

Juice of ½ lemon

½ pineapple, skin removed, cored, and cut into equal-sized pieces

4 strawberries

4 black grapes

1½ tablespoons butter

1 tablespoon sugar

1 tablespoon honey

Preheat the oven to 350°F.

Sprinkle the apple with the lemon juice to stop it from discoloring. Thread the pineapple, apple, strawberries, and grapes onto skewers. (If you are using wooden skewers, soak them for an hour in water before use to prevent them from charring or burning.)

Melt the butter in the cast iron dish in the oven. Sprinkle the sugar and honey into the dish, mix well, and return to the oven for 10 minutes until you have a light caramel.

Remove from the oven and place the fruit kebabs in the dish. Roll the skewers in the caramel until coated.

Heat the broiler to medium-high. Place the fruit kebabs under the broiler and cook for 2 minutes until starting to color.

Serve the fruit kebabs with a scoop of vanilla ice cream and a strawberry coulis, if you like.

FLAMBÉED FRUIT
WITH SOUR CREAM

Sweet, sour, and simply divine!

10-inch Stoneware Pie Dish

SERVES 4
Preparation time: 15 minutes
Cooking time: 20 minutes

1½ tablespoons butter

6 figs, cut in half

3 plums, pitted and cut in half

16 cherries, pitted

¼ cup sugar

3 tablespoons Grand Marnier

1 small handful of mint leaves, to decorate

½ cup sour cream or crème fraîche, to serve

Preheat the oven to 400°F.

Grease the stoneware pie dish with the butter.

Arrange the figs, plums, and cherries in the dish and sprinkle them with the sugar. Place in the oven for 20 minutes until softened.

Remove the dish from the oven and flambé at the table with the Grand Marnier.

Decorate the fruit with the mint leaves and serve with sour cream or crème fraîche on the side.

Round Skillet Grill

SERVES 6
Preparation time: 10 minutes, plus marinating
Cooking time: 15 minutes

HONEYED FIG BRUSCHETTA
A sweet bruschetta is an exciting twist on the more usual savory version.

⅓ cup olive oil

3 tablespoons balsamic vinegar

¼ cup honey, divided

12 fresh figs, cut in half

Butter, for spreading

6 slices of bread

Freshly ground black pepper

Chopped mint leaves, to decorate

Sour cream, to serve

Add the oil, vinegar, and 2 tablespoons of the honey to a bowl and stir to combine. Season with pepper.

Place the figs cut-side down in the dressing, drizzle with more dressing to coat, and let marinate for 10 minutes, occasionally basting them in the dressing.

Heat the skillet grill over medium heat. Butter the slices of bread and grill the bread in the skillet until toasted and golden brown. (You may need to cook them in two batches.) Remove the toast from the skillet grill and set aside.

Place the figs in the skillet grill and cook for 3 minutes, turning occasionally, until soft.

Spoon the sour cream onto the grilled toast followed by the warm figs. Drizzle with the remaining dressing and honey and decorate with mint.

2-quart Round Dutch Oven

SERVES 6
Preparation time: 10 minutes
Cooking time: 10 minutes

BERRY SOUP WITH LEMON THYME

Serve this jewel-colored fruit "soup" with a spoonful of mascarpone and a sprig of fresh mint.

1¼ lb fresh or frozen mixed berries, including raspberries, red currants, blueberries, and strawberries

1 cup water, or 3 tablespoons if using frozen fruit

¼ cup packed soft light brown sugar

1 vanilla bean, split lengthwise

Juice of 1 lime

5 lemon thyme sprigs

Prepare the fresh fruit, if using, by removing any stalks or stems and cutting the strawberries into pieces, if large.

Pour the measured water into the Dutch oven (or add 3 tablespoons if using frozen fruit), then add the sugar, vanilla bean, lime juice, and lemon thyme. Stir and cook the fruit over medium heat for 10 minutes, or until the sugar dissolves and the fruit is soft.

Keep warm or let cool and chill until ready to serve.

To serve, spoon the soup into shallow bowls. Top each serving with a spoonful of mascarpone and scatter with chopped mint.

RICE PUDDING WITH LEMON & CINNAMON

A fresh take on a classic favorite.

2-quart Tagine

SERVES 4
Preparation time: 10 minutes
Cooking time: 35 minutes

4 cups whole milk

Seeds from 1 vanilla bean

1 cinnamon stick

1 cup long-grain rice, rinsed and drained

⅔ cup superfine sugar

Grated zest of ½ lemon

3 tablespoons butter, diced

¼ cup unsalted shelled pistachios, chopped

Pour the milk into bottom of the tagine and add the vanilla seeds and cinnamon. Bring the mixture to a simmer over medium-low heat.

Add the rice to the milk and return to a simmer.

Reduce the heat to low, cover with the lid, and cook for about 30 minutes, or until the rice is cooked. Stir regularly to prevent the rice from sticking to the bottom.

Stir the sugar, lemon zest, and butter into the rice until combined.

Serve the rice pudding scattered with the pistachios.

**Square Skillet Grill
with Double Handles**

SERVES 6
Preparation time: 5 minutes
Cooking time: 10 minutes

GRILLED BRIOCHE WITH BRIE, RHUBARB & PISTACHIOS

A delicious variation on traditional French toast.

3 eggs

2 tablespoons milk

6 slices of brioche,
cut in half diagonally

1½ tablespoons butter

5½ oz Brie cheese, sliced

1 lemon, cut in half

⅓ cup rhubarb chutney

½ cup pistachios, finely chopped

Beat the eggs with the milk in a shallow dish. Dip the slices of brioche into the mixture and drain off any excess.

Heat the skillet grill over medium heat and grease liberally with some of the butter. Grill the bread on one side until golden brown. Turn the bread over and place a slice of Brie on top and chargrill until golden brown and the cheese has melted slightly. Cook the bread in batches, adding more butter when needed.

Squeeze some lemon juice over the bread and melted cheese. Top with a spoonful of rhubarb chutney and pistachios before serving.

2-quart Round Dutch Oven

BRIOCHE WITH POPPY SEEDS

A delicious enriched loaf with a hint of honey and a poppy seed topping—and it's cooked in a Dutch oven!

MAKES: 1 LOAF
Preparation time: 25 minutes, plus rising
Cooking time: 40 minutes

1½ lb strong white bread flour, plus extra for dusting

2 teaspoons salt

3 tablespoons poppy seeds, divided

1½ teaspoons (¼-oz packet) active dry yeast

1 cup lukewarm water

4 eggs, lightly beaten, divided

2 tablespoons honey

½ cup sunflower oil, plus extra for greasing

Mix the flour, salt, 2 tablespoons of the poppy seeds, and the active dry yeast in a large mixing bowl and make a well in the middle. Add the measured water followed by 3 of the eggs, honey, and sunflower oil. Using a large spatula, start to mix the liquid ingredients gently together, then gradually take up the flour, starting in the middle and working your way outward. Once the mixture has come together into a dough, turn it out onto a well floured surface.

Knead the dough with well floured hands for at least 10 minutes until smooth and elastic.

Grease the Dutch oven with a little oil and dust with flour. Place the dough in the Dutch oven, cover with a dish cloth, and place in a warm, dry place. Let the dough rise for 1½ hours, or until it has doubled in size. You can also let it rise in a cool place for a longer period of time.

Preheat the oven to 425°F.

Brush the reserved egg over the risen brioche, then sprinkle the top with the remaining poppy seeds. Bake the brioche for 10 minutes, then reduce the oven to 375°F and continue to bake for a further 30 minutes until risen and golden. Let cool slightly in the Dutch oven, then turn out and serve warm with butter.

INDEX

A

ale
  a classic beef casserole 11
  duck with glazed turnips 82
  lamb navarin 48
  pork cheeks in dark ale 45
  turkey and apricots in ale 72

almonds
  almond pudding with pink grapefruit 195
  baked sea bass in salt crust 109
  caramelized pineapple with kirsch 196
  lamb with prunes, almonds, and honey 54
  spiced squash with raisins 177

amaretti cookies: grilled peaches with Amaretto & amaretti crisp 198

anchovies
  pork chops in rosé with rosemary and anchovies 29
  stuffed herb chicken with cherry tomatoes 63
  zucchini and anchovy bruschetta 122

aniseed, bacon-wrapped trout with fennel and 121

apples
  caramelized orchard fruit with Calvados sauce 187
  chicken with caramelized apples 60
  five-spice and vanilla poached apples 189
  sticky fruit kebabs 205
  tarte tatin 191

apricots
  lamb with apricots, raisins, and chickpeas 46
  South African seafood stew 93
  turkey and apricots in ale 72

artichokes: Italian braised vegetables 168

arugula
  lobster with Moroccan spices 132
  risotto with a trio of cheeses 143

Asian salad 14, 112

asparagus
  asparagus with saffron cream 172
  eggs en cocotte with asparagus 153
  spring vegetable casserole 146

B

bacon
  bacon-wrapped trout with fennel and aniseed 121
  coq au vin blanc 58
  herb-stuffed pigeon with grapes 77
  sausages with white beans, red bell pepper, and saffron 41

basil: eggplant, pesto, and mozzarella stacks 162

bean sprouts
  Asian salad 14, 112
  oriental-spiced beef 17
  salmon fillets with Asian salad 112

beans
  cassoulet 42
  sausages with white beans, red bell pepper, and saffron 41

beef
  a classic beef casserole 11
  ginger-soy chargrilled steak 14
  Lebanese-style meatballs 24
  oriental-spiced beef 17
  pot-au-feu maison 12

beer: a classic beef casserole 11
  duck with glazed turnips 82
  lamb navarin 48
  pork cheeks in dark ale 45
  turkey and apricots in ale 72

beets: duck legs with beets and caraway 81

Belgian chicken pie with lime and tarragon pesto 67

Belgian endives: braised Belgian endives with honey and orange 179

bell peppers
  Mediterranean sausage casserole 39
  monkfish with olives and new potatoes 105
  Provençal roasted vegetables 171
  rice with Mediterranean vegetables 145
  roasting bell peppers 151
  sausages with white beans, red bell pepper, and saffron 41
  Spanish chorizo with eggs and Manchego 36
  spiced roasted bell pepper soup 151
  sweet bell peppers with eggs 155

berries
  berry soup with lemon thyme 210
  caramelized pineapple with kirsch 196

blood oranges with Campari and honey 193

bread
  brioche with poppy seeds 217
  grilled brioche with Brie, rhubarb, and pistachios 214
  honey fig bruschetta 208
  zucchini and anchovy bruschetta 122

Brie: grilled brioche with Brie, rhubarb, and pistachios 214

brioche
  brioche with poppy seeds 217
  grilled brioche with Brie, rhubarb, and pistachios 214

brochettes
  duck, prune, and orange brochettes 85
  herb-crusted turkey brochettes 71
  rabbit brochettes with sage and lemon 87
  swordfish, chorizo, and sun-dried tomato brochettes 102

broth: oriental-spiced beef 17

bruschetta
  honey fig bruschetta 208
  zucchini and anchovy bruschetta 122

Brussels sprouts: pot-au-feu maison 12

bulgur wheat: spring vegetable casserole 146

butternut squash
  pot-au-feu maison 12
  spiced squash with raisins 177

C

Calvados
  caramelized orchard fruit with Calvados sauce 187
  guinea fowl with pears and hard cider 75

Campari: blood oranges with Campari and honey 193

capers
  eggplant salsa 165
  pistachio-crusted cod with tomatoes and capers 96
  stuffed herb chicken with cherry tomatoes 63

caraway, duck legs with beets and 81

carrots
  Asian salad 14
  a classic beef casserole 11
  creamy veal ragout 23
  duck legs with beets and caraway 81

An Hachette UK Company
www.hachette.co.uk

First published in Great Britain in 2016
by Mitchell Beazley,
a division of Octopus Publishing Group Ltd
Carmelite House, 50 Victoria Embankment
London EC4Y 0DZ
www.octopusbooksusa.com

Distributed in the US by
Hachette Book Group
1290 Avenue of the Americas
4th and 5th Floors
New York, NY 10020

Distributed in Canada by
Canadian Manda Group
664 Annette St.
Toronto, Ontario, Canada M6S 2C8

ISBN 978 1 78472 237 1

Printed and bound in China

10 9 8 7 6 5 4 3 2 1

Publisher: Alison Starling
Designer: Jaz Bahra
Design: Bold & Noble
Assistant Editor: Ella Parsons
Copy Editor: Nicola Graimes
Senior Production Manager: Katherine Hockley

Use fresh herbs, unsalted butter and medium-sized eggs
unless otherwise stated. This book contains dishes made
with lightly cooked eggs. It is prudent for more vulnerable
people such as pregnant and nursing mothers, invalids,
the elderly, babies, and young children to avoid uncooked
or lightly cooked eggs.